The Early Modern Englishwoman:
A Facsimile Library of Essential Works

Series I

Printed Writings, 1500–1640: Part 2

Volume 2

Brief Confessional Writings:
Grey, Stubbes, Livingstone, Clarksone

The Early Modern Englishwoman:
A Facsimile Library of Essential Works

Series I

Printed Writings, 1500–1640: Part 2

Volume 2

Brief Confessional Writings:
Grey, Stubbes, Livingstone and Clarksone

Selected and Introduced by
Mary Ellen Lamb

General Editors
Betty S. Travitsky and Patrick Cullen

Ashgate

Aldershot • Burlington USA • Singapore • Sydney

The Introductory Note copyright © Mary Ellen Lamb 2001

Published by
Ashgate Publishing Limited
Gower House
Croft Road
Aldershot
Hants GU11 3HR
England

Ashgate Publishing Company
131 Main Street
Burlington, VT 05401-5600 USA

Ashgate website: http://www.ashgate.com

British Library Cataloguing-in-Publication Data
The early modern Englishwoman : a facsimile library of
    essential works.
    Part 2 : Printed writings, 1500–1640 : Vol. 2
    1. English literature – Early modern, 1500–1700   2. English
    literature – Women authors   3. Women – England – History –
    Renaissance, 1450–1600 – Sources   4. Women – England
    History – Modern period, 1600– – Sources   5. Women – Literary
    collections
    I. Dudley, Jane   II. Travitsky, Betty S.   III. Cullen, Patrick
    Colborn   IV. Lamb, Mary Ellen
    820.8'09287

Library of Congress Cataloging-in-Publication Data
The early modern Englishwoman: a facsimile library of essential works. Part 2. Printed Writings, 1500–1640 / general editors, Betty S. Travitsky and Patrick Cullen.

See page vi for complete CIP Block 99–54550

The woodcut reproduced on the title page and on the case is from the title page of Margaret Roper's trans. of [Desiderius Erasmus] *A Devout Treatise upon the Pater Noster* (circa 1524).

ISBN 1 84014 215 4

Printed in Great Britain by Antony Rowe Ltd, Chippenham, Wiltshire

CONTENTS

Library of Congress Cataloging-in-Publication Data
Brief confessional writings: Grey, Stubbes, Livingstone, and Clarksone /
selected and introduced by Mary Ellen Lamb.
     p. cm. -- (The early modern Englishwoman. Printed writings, 1500–1640, Part 2 ; v. 2)
  Contents: The communication had betwene the Lady Iane and Fecknam ; A letter of the
Lady Iane sent vnto her father ; An other Letter of the Lady Iane to M.H. ; A Letter
written by the Lady Iane … vnto her sister Lady Katherine ; A certayne effectuall prayer ;
Wordes that the Lady Iane spake vpon the scaffolde; Certayne prety verses wrytten by
the sayd Lady Iane wyth a pynne / Jane Grey Dudley -- A moste heavenly confession of
the Christian faith ; A moste wonderfull conflict betwixt Sathan and her soule / Katherine Emmes
Stubbes -- The Confession and Conversion / Eleanor Hay Livingstone -- The Conflict in
Conscience of a deare Christian / Bessie Clarksone.
  ISBN 1-84014-215-4
  1. Protestant women--England--Biography. 2. Protestant women--Scotland--Biography.
I. Lamb, Mary Ellen. II. Grey, Jane, Lady, 1537–1554. Communication had betwene the
Lady Iane and Fecknam. III. Grey, Jane, Lady, 1537–1554. A letter of the Lady Iane sent
vnto her father. IV. Grey, Jane, Lady, 1537–1554. An other Letter of the Lady Iane to M.H.
V. Grey, Jane, Lady, 1537–1554. A Letter written by the Lady Iane … vnto her Sister Lady
Katherine. VI. Grey, Jane, Lady, 1537–1554. A Certayne effectuall prayer. VII. Grey, Jane,
Lady, 1537–1554. Wordes that the Lady Iane spake vpon the scaffolde. VIII. Grey, Jane,
Lady, 1537–1554. Certayne prety verses wrytten by the sayd Lady Iane wyth a pynne.
IX. Stubbes, Katherine, 1570 or 71–1590. A moste heavenly confession of the Christian
faith. X. Stubbes, Katherine, 1570 or 71–1590. A moste wonderfull conflict betwixt Sathan
and her soule. XI. Livingstone, Eleanor, Countess of Linlithgow, b. 1552. The Confession and
Conversion. XII. Clarksone, Bessie, d. 1625. The Conflict in Conscience of a deare Christian.
XIII. Series.

BR317 .B75 2000
274.2'06--dc21

                                                  99–54550

PREFACE
BY THE GENERAL EDITORS

Until very recently, scholars of the early modern period have assumed that there were no Judith Shakespeares in early modern England. Much of the energy of the current generation of scholars has been devoted to constructing a history of early modern England that takes into account what women actually wrote, what women actually read, and what women actually did. In so doing the masculinist representation of early modern women, both in their own time and ours, is deconstructed. The study of early modern women has thus become one of the most important—indeed perhaps the most important—means for the rewriting of early modern history.

The Early Modern Englishwoman: A Facsimile Library of Essential Works is one of the developments of this energetic reappraisal of the period. As the names on our advisory board and our list of editors testify, it has been the beneficiary of scholarship in the field, and we hope it will also be an essential part of that scholarship's continuing momentum.

The Early Modern Englishwoman is designed to make available a comprehensive and focused collection of writings in English from 1500 to 1750, both by women and for and about them. The three series of *Printed Writings* (1500–1640, 1641–1700, and 1701–1750) provide a comprehensive if not entirely complete collection of the separately published writings by women. In reprinting these writings we intend to remedy one of the major obstacles to the advancement of feminist criticism of the early modern period, namely the limited availability of the very texts upon which the field is based. The volumes in the facsimile library reproduce carefully chosen copies of these texts, incorporating significant variants (usually in appendices). Each text is preceded by a short introduction providing an overview of the life and work of a writer along with a survey of important scholarship. These works, we strongly believe, deserve a large readership—of historians, literary critics, feminist critics, and non-specialist readers.

The Early Modern Englishwoman also includes separate facsimile series of *Essential Works for the Study of Early Modern Women* and of *Manuscript Writings*. These facsimile series are complemented by *The Early Modern Englishwoman 1500–1750: Contemporary Editions*. Also under our general editorship, this series will include both old-spelling and modernized editions of works by and about women and gender in early modern England.

New York City
2001

INTRODUCTORY NOTE

The selections below by Lady Jane Grey Dudley, Katherine Emmes Stubbes, Eleanor Hay Livingstone, and Bessie Clarksone are 'confessional' in the sense that they witness religious doctrines. As confessions of Protestant faith by women across a range of classes, from queen to commoner, they suggest the diversity of subjectivities possible to Reformation subjects. This diversity is all the more notable because these women share an awareness of approaching death, whether from execution, illness or old age; and their confessions delineate specifically Calvinist versions of the *ars moriendi* (art of dying) tradition. Since many passages emphasize recitations of Protestant doctrine, these selections do not, on the surface, resemble 'confessions' in the more modern sense of intimate disclosures. Yet, to some extent, the distinction between these two meanings of 'confession' blurs in a paradox at the core of these texts. The value of a confession of faith lies not in its originality, as in a traditionally 'authored' writing, but in its conformity to prescribed dogma, often expressed by paraphrasing or reproducing an approved text. For this reason, words and phrases from prior texts echo resoundingly through much of this volume, and whole sections of the transcribed words of Stubbes and Livingstone, in particular, represent close paraphrases of Protestant tenets. It is a paradox, that even the direct recitation of the words written by another – of a confession of faith, of a Psalm, of the Lord's Prayer – may number among the most deeply felt forms of personal self-expression. Especially within religious experience, the 'I believe' of the speaker may fervently inhabit the 'I believe' of a written text.

For the most part, these works were never intended as acts of individual and authentic self-expression. Except for the writings of Lady Jane Grey Dudley, these selections consist of oral transcriptions generated through collaborations with male transcribers who may have intervened in the texts. The pious deathbed speeches of Katherine Emmes Stubbes were reported by her husband Philip. Disavowing Catholicism, Eleanor Hay Livingstone signed her name to articles of Protestant faith she declaimed before witnesses. Minister William Livingstone published a dialogue recording Bessie Clarksone's lengthy crisis of faith under his name. Of more importance than the absolute veracity of these transcriptions is the cultural significance of associating these particular texts with these particular women. The publication and marketing of these selections as spoken by women demonstrate the significance of women's voices, and specifically the voices of these women, to contemporaries. The specific ideological tasks advanced by the representation of these women as speaking these words varied according to historical circumstance and intended audiences. The range in class status among these women indicates efforts to appeal to diverse social groups. Declared Queen of England by a Protestant faction who held out briefly against the Catholic Mary Tudor, Lady Jane Grey Dudley composed her writings shortly before her execution. Dudley's writings gain enormous political, as well as religious, power through her martyrdom, at the age of seventeen, for the Protestant cause. Addressed especially to the 'ignorant and wilfull Papists of this land,' the confession of Protestant doctrine by the aged Eleanor Hay Livingstone, wealthy Countess of Linlithgow, patterned an action desired particularly for the prominent Catholic aristocrats of Scotland. In addition to witnessing Protestant doctrine, Katherine Emmes Stubbes modelled a form of wifehood among the middling sort. Her husband's description of her avid reading of Scripture in constant consultation with him ('How expound you this place?' A2ᵛ), simultaneously signified religious zeal, wifely deference, and contempt for the worldly goods increasingly available in London. Showing no such evidence of wide reading, the dialogue between Bessie Clarksone and her minister models strategies for clergy counselling parishioners convinced of their unworthiness of God's grace. This volume illustrates that, rather than silencing women, the Protestant Reformation drew upon women's speech to serve a range of ideological functions.

In addition to Protestant doctrine, the confessions of these four women share a sense of impending death, whether by execution, old age, or illness. Exonerating these women from any desire to gain worldly influence, approaching death also bestows a form of godly subjectivity as these women participate in an *ars moriendi* tradition. The words particularly of Stubbes and Clarksone outline a specifically Calvinist orientation. Since for Calvinists the spiritual fate of elect and reprobate alike was predestined, the battle between angels and devils for the soul of *moriens*, according to the medieval Catholic custom, was no longer appropriate. For Calvinists, a good death revealed *moriens'* calm 'assurance' as a sign of election. Lady Jane Grey Dudley displayed no apparent hesitation over her election. Especially for later Calvinists, however, true assurance was to be hard won in the fate of doubts (Lake 158), and so the Calvinist *ars moriendi* adapted this earlier deathbed battle to involve *moriens* and despair, often personified by Satan. Katherine Stubbes' 'A moste wonderfull conflict betwixt Sathan and her soule' models her triumph over despair that she was 'a sinner, and therefore shall be dammed' (C3). The proper balance between despair and faith was not always so easily determined. In a related account, Katherine Brettergh's intense anxiety over her election gave her Catholic neighbors 'occasion to report' her religion 'comfortles' and her death 'despairing' (06v) (Warnicke and Doebler). Bessie Clarksone's lengthy struggle against despair for the three and a half years before her death occupies most of the speeches attributed to her. Denied a victorious affirmation of faith when 'her words ... failed her' (41), she could only signify her assurance by raising her eyes. While the possible intervention of male transcribers must not be underestimated, the range among these narratives provides a sense of the diverse ways in which the doctrine of assurance may have become translated into the subjectivities of Protestant women.

Lady Jane Grey Dudley

As the ruler of England for nine days, Lady Jane Grey Dudley (1537–1554), is by far the best-known of the authors in this volume. The granddaughter of Mary Tudor, younger sister of Henry VIII, Jane Grey was married in 1553 to Guilford Dudley, son of the powerful John Dudley, Duke of Northumberland, as part of a scheme to place her on the throne at the death of Edward VI. (We style her here as Lady Jane Grey, as she is best known.) Partly to prevent the religious turmoil attending the accession of the Catholic Mary Tudor, Edward VI agreed to set aside his sisters and declare the sixteen-year-old Jane Grey his heir. Despite her own initial resistance, on 10 July 1553 Jane Grey was declared Queen of England by her supporters. Nine days later, the Duke of Northumberland's troops were defeated and Mary Tudor assumed the English throne. Jane Grey was arraigned for high treason on 14 November and executed on 12 February 1554. Of the many biographies of Jane Grey, Hester W. Chapman's is one of the most rigorously tied to historical sources.

The Lady Jane was remarkable for her classical learning. Tutored by the humanist John Aylmer, she became fluent in Latin and possibly Greek, and she wrote learned letters to Henry Bullinger in Zurich. Roger Ascham's *Schoolmaster* records her preference for reading Plato's *Phaedo* to hunting game with her family.

The first printed reports of the writings and speeches of Jane Grey before her death are recorded in John Foxe's *Actes and Monumentes*, which ran through nine editions from 1563 to 1684. Including 'A letter of the Lady Iane sent vnto her Father' and marginal notes, the 1570 edition is more complete than the 1563 edition, but less corrupt than subsequent editions. The 1570 edition (Volume 2, Book 10, pp. 1580–1585) held at The Folger Library is reproduced in this volume for the items by Jane Grey.

'The communication had betwene the Lady IANE and FECKNAM'

Sent by Queen Mary to convert Jane Grey to Catholicism, John Feckenham elicits from her the following central tenets of the Protestant faith: Christians are justified by faith rather than by works, baptism and the Lord's supper are the only two sacraments, the bread and wine of the eucharist are not composed of the actual body and blood of Christ, and Scripture rather than Church tradition is the only valid basis for belief. This communication is notable for its dramatic representation of Lady Jane and Feckenham. Displaying absolute confidence in her answers to complex theological questions, Lady Jane sometimes even assumes the rhetorical position of interrogator. To Feckenham's expressed belief in seven sacraments, she asks, 'By what scripture finde you that?' The Feckenham of this communication fumbles, replying, 'Wel, we wil talke of that hereafter.' This dialogue portrays Jane Grey as the winner of this debate.

'A letter of the Lady Iane sent vnto her Father'

Clearly assigning blame to her father for her imminent execution, Lady Jane forcefully asserts her innocence of any desire to reign. She had assumed the monarchy of England only because she had been 'constrained' and 'continually assayed'. At the same time, she comforts her father by assuring him that she welcomes her death and the heavenly joys it will bring her. She prays for his soul, so that they will meet again in heaven.

'An other Letter of the Lady Iane to M.H., late Chaplayne to the Duke of Suffolke her father, and then fallen from the truth of Gods most holy worde'

In the 1563 edition, Foxe does not include the initials of this man, whose name he claims was 'knowen' to him; the 1583 edition supplies this name in the heading as 'M. Harding'. This relatively long letter uses military terms to castigate the chaplain as a 'white livered milkesop' who fled the position assigned by his 'chief captaine Christ'. Explaining the gravity of his sinful backsliding, Jane Grey also promises him God's forgiveness if he returns to Christ's true religion. In addition to eloquence, she also relies on numerous citations from Scripture for her argument.

'A Letter written by the Lady Iane in the ende of the new Testament in Greeke, the which she sent vnto her Sister Lady Katherine, the nyght before she suffered'

Describing her gift of a New Testament to her sister as more valuable than jewels, Jane Grey praises spiritual treasures over worldly ones. A book to pattern the Christian life, it shall 'teach you to live, and learne you to dye'. This letter became part of an *ars moriendi* literature when appended to the third of the four 'Books of Death' that make up Otto Werdmueller's undated 'A moste frutefull piththye and learned treatise, how a christen man ought to behave himself' (*STC* 25251). Her letter to her sister and 'A certayne effectuall prayer' were printed as examples of model devotional literature by and for women in Thomas Bentley's 1582 compilation, *A Monument of Matrones*.

'A certayne effectuall prayer'

In this passionate prayer reminiscent of Christ's prayer at Gethsemane, the Lady Jane begs not to be tempted above her powers. She asks either to be delivered, as were the Israelites from Pharaoh, or else to be given grace to bear her miseries with patience. In an extended metaphor, she asks God to arm her with the shield of faith. Finally, she refers herself entirely to God's will.

'Wordes that the Lady Iane spake vpon the scaffolde at the houre of her death'

In the tradition of scaffold speeches, Jane Grey upheld the law by admitting the unlawfulness of her consenting to reign as queen, but she denied any desire or any attempt on her part to have attained the throne. Reciting a psalm, divesting herself of garments, forgiving the hangman, the Lady Jane maintained dignified control, only asking 'What shall I do?' when, after being blindfolded, she could not find the block. This scaffold scene was included in Richard Grafton's *Chronicle* (1569), which omits a brief interaction with Feckenham and excuses her for her ignorance of the law and her trust in false council concerning her claim to the throne. Raphael Holinshed's *Chronicles* (1578) follows Grafton. John Stow's *Chronicles of England* (1580) does not include her death speech in his description of her execution.

'Certayne prety verses wrytten by the sayd Lady Iane wyth a pynne'

The 1563 edition translates these verses in this way: 'Do never thinke it straunge, / Though now I have misfortune, / For if that fortune chaunge, / The same to thee may happen.' The second verse reads as follows: 'If God do helpe thee, / Hate shall not hurte thee, / If God do fayle thee, / Then shall not labour prevayle thee. / Post tenebras spero lucem.' [After the shadows I hope for light.]

Jane Grey's writings were soon excerpted from Foxe's *Actes and Monumentes* and published on their own. The items published in the 1563 *Actes and Monumentes* were entered in the Stationers' Register in 1569–1570 as 'An epistle of the ladye Jane to a learned man of late falne', omitting the heading to the Harding letter, twenty-six lines of courteous exchange with Feckenham, and including an abbreviated and somewhat garbled version of her scaffold speech. Another undated and untitled version of this edition appeared, with a revised scaffold speech and a prayer by John Knox. In 1615, this 1569–1570 edition was somewhat expanded and printed with the title, *The life, death and actions of the lady Jane Gray. Containing foure discourses written with her owne hands.* This work became popular, to be published again in 1629 and 1636. Two other histories which include words of uncertain authenticity are Michelangelo Florio, *Historia de la vita ... Giovanna Graia* (Middelburg: R. Pittore, 1607), 60, 76 and Francis Godwin, *Annales of England* (1630), 294–97. Additional manuscript material includes Harleian MS 2342 (Jane Grey's prayer book), with an additional letter to her father, a note to the lieutenant of the Tower, and an inscription in Latin, Greek, and English. Harleian MS 194, an anonymous pocket diary since published for the Camden Society, records a dinner conversation with Jane Grey at the Tower on 29 August 1553. The Lady Jane's works are quoted in the many biographies of her life, as well in recent anthologies of writings by early modern women. 'A certayne prayer', part of her dialogue with Feckenham, and her words spoken at her death have been included in various anthologies, such as *The Paradise of Women*, 41–44. Her discussion with Ascham and her words on the scaffold appear in the sixth edition of *The Norton Anthology of English Literature*, 993, 996.

Katherine Emmes Stubbes

Most available information concerning Katherine Emmes Stubbes (1571?–1590) is contained in her husband Philip's *A Christall Glasse for Christian Women*. Reproduced here in its entirety, the work describes her pious life and records her words and actions at her death. The biographical forepart serves as an introduction to her detailed and learned confession of Protestant dogma on her deathbed and her spiritual victory over Satan, who attempted to reduce her to despair of God's forgiveness of her sins.

Living in London for many years, Katherine Emmes' parents were 'honest and wealthie' (A2). Her father was 'of a sound religion', while her mother was 'religious and also zealous' (A2). Her father had 'borne divers Offices of worship' (A2), and her mother was a 'Dutchwoman'. At the age of fifteen, after her father's death, Katherine Emmes married Philip Stubbes, perhaps best known for his attack on theater in his *Anatomy of Abuses*. After four-and-a-half years, she gave birth to a boy and about two weeks later she contracted a 'burning quotidian Ague' (A3v), in which she lingered for several weeks until she died.

Stubbes' account of his wife's actions and words during the years of their marriage and during her last illness provides a Protestant model for women facing ordinary deaths rather than martyrdom. It also represents her as a model of conduct by which to lead an unworldly life. Refusing the superficial pleasures of rich food or strong drink, beautiful garments, scurrilous talk or swearing, and outings with her women friends to plays or interludes, she had devoted herself instead to the reading of scripture under the supervision of her husband, to whom she had adapted her every word and mood. When, in turn, two weeks after giving birth to a boy, she fell ill for about six weeks before she died, her husband recorded her various speeches abjuring the world and desiring to die into everlasting life.

'A moste heavenly confession of the Christian faith' (sigs. B1v–C3)

Beginning with an exposition of the Trinity and proceeding to describe in more detail the nature of God the father and then of God the son, Katherine Stubbes' confession loosely follows the Apostle's Creed of the Anglican Church, with additions to distinguish her beliefs from such Roman Catholic tenets as salvation through good works, purgatory, transubstantiation, and the intercession of the saints. Her belief in predestination was in conformity with the Calvinist orientation of the Anglican Church of that time. She concludes with a declaration that the dead would know one another in heaven.

Katherine Stubbes' dry recitation demonstrated the importance of belief in correct doctrine as a sign of election. Her ability to elaborate on different doctrines also revealed a pronounced intellectual side to this Calvinist ideal for women. Incorporating the density of written prose, the complexity of her transcribed speech patterns makes it probable that her husband edited at least her phrasing, and possibly the content as well.

'A moste wonderfull conflict betwixt Sathan and her soule' (sigs. C3–C4v)

Katherine Stubbes' final victory over worldly temptation is recounted as a dramatic encounter between herself and Satan in which she thoroughly bested her opponent. Her confrontation with Satan introduces the problem of assurance, not entirely resolved in the Calvinist branch of the Protestant faith.

A Christall Glasse for Christian Women was a phenomenal best-seller. First published in 1591, it went through thirty-five editions by 1695. This volume reproduces the 1606 edition held at The British Library for the following reasons: The 1591 edition is blotted and lacks a title page. The cleaner 1592 edition makes about sixty changes, a number of which are substantive, but it omits a twenty-line passage restored in subsequent editions. The 1603 text, which judiciously draws on both the 1591 and the 1592 texts for emendations, is marred by blotches and dark spots; this is the only text which describes Stubbes as nineteen years of age at her death instead of twenty. The 1606 edition, which is a clean text, follows the 1603 text closely in most places, although choosing the 1591 over the 1592 text in a couple of places where the 1603 does not. After this edition, the texts become increasingly corrupt, becoming fairly standardized by 1626.

Excerpts from this work have been published in *The Paradise of Women*, 45–46.

Eleanor Hay Livingstone

Eleanor Hay was born in 1552 to Andrew Hay, eighth Earl of Erroll. When she was married to Alexander Livingstone, seventh Baron Livingstone and first Earl of Linlithgow, in 1584, the parish records list her name as 'Helenor' Hay (IGI), which accounts for her name 'Helen Livingston' attributed as the author of *The Confession and Conversion* by the STC. With her brother Francis, who became ninth Earl of Erroll, she was converted to the Catholic religion by her relative Edward Hay, a Jesuit priest. Her Catholic faith posed a difficulty to the Church of Scotland when James VI gave the care of his daughter, Princess Elizabeth (later Princess of Bohemia) to the Livingstones, who raised her from 1596 until 1603 when James succeeded to the English throne. When the Church objected to his choice, James replied that he had not entrusted his daughter to Lady Livingstone, but to her husband. By 1606, Eleanor Livingstone had renounced the Catholic religion.

The Confession and Conversion of the Right Honorable, Most Illustrious, and Elect Lady my Lady C. of L.

Rather than a deathbed confession, this work, demonstrating the countess's conversion from Catholicism to the reformed Church of Scotland, was written in her 'old dayes' (B2) and published to be read 'of all' including the 'wilfull Papists of this land'. Beginning with a psalm and ending with more psalms and a prayer, the majority of this work is taken up with listing and renouncing thirteen specific doctrines distinguishing the Catholic from the Protestant religion. All but one of these (the renunciation of the Catholic command to abstain from meats) were included in the 'A general confession' prefatory to the 1581 *Confession of the true and christian fayth* (*STC* 22022), a document central to the evolving Church of Scotland. The 1629 publication of this work represented a timely contribution to the Scottish resistance to the attempts by Charles I to impose the Anglican faith on the predominantly Presbyterian Scotland after his accession and marriage to a Catholic wife in 1625. The only extant copy of *The Confession and Conversion of the Right Honorable, Most Illustrious, and Elect Lady my Lady C. of L.* (1629), held at The Huntington Library, is reproduced in this volume.

Bessie Clarksone

Little is known of Bessie Clarksone except that she died in Lanerk parish in Scotland in April 1625 (*The Conflict in Conscience*, sig. B11). The *IGI* lists the birth of an Elizabeth Clarkson in Lanerk about 1584, who may be the same person.

The Conflict in Conscience of a deare Christian

This work consists of dialogues taking place over a three-and-a-half-year period between Clarksone and her pastor William Livingstone, under whose name it is listed in the *STC*. Doubts similar to those voiced by Stubbes represent the primary topic of this text. *The Conflict in Conscience* may well function, in fact, as a model for ministers more than for dying women, for Clarksone continually meets W.L.'s patient reassurances with despairing disbelief. Absent at her death, W.L. depends on the word of 'diverse witnesse' (sig. B11) who describe her lifting her eyes to heaven to express her 'victorious faith' (B11v). Never explicitly resolved 'out of her owne mouth' (B11), this lengthy record of Clarksone's spiritual struggle remains the most problematic in this collection.

Despite the claim on its title-page that it was 'newly corrected and amended' and despite W.L.'s prefatory letter stating that an imperfect copy had jumbled his words with Clarksone's, only one edition is known. The only extant copy, held at The British Library, of *The Conflict in Conscience of a deare Christian, named Bessie Clarksone in the Parish of Lanerk, which shee lay under three years & an half, with the conference that past betwixt her Pastor and her at divers times* (1631), is reproduced here. An excerpt from this work has been published in *The Paradise of Women* (47–8).

References

STC 11223 [Foxe, including Grey Dudley]; *STC* 16610 [Livingstone]; *STC* 16611 [Clarksone]; *STC* 23383 [Stubbes]
Ascham, Roger (1967), *The Schoolmaster* (ed.) Lawrence V. Ryan, Ithaca: Cornell University Press
Chapman, Hester W. (1962), *Lady Jane Grey*, Boston: Little, Brown
Cokayne, George Edward (1932), 'Livingstone', 'Linlithgow', *The Complete Peerage*, VIII, London: St. Catherine Press
Henderson, Thomas Finlayson (1917), 'Francis Hay', 'Alexander Livingstone', *Dictionary of National Biographer*, Oxford: Oxford University Press
International Genealogical Index (1988), Salt Lake City, UT: Family History Department of the Church of Jesus Christ of Latter-Day Saints
King, John (1982), *English Reformation Literature: The Tudor Origins of the Protestant Tradition*, Princeton: Princeton University Press
Lake, Peter (1982), *Moderate Puritans and the Elizabethan Church*, Cambridge: Cambridge University Press
Levin, Carole (1985), 'Lady Jane Grey: Protestant Queen and Martyr', in Margaret Hannay (ed.), *Silent But for the Word*, Kent, OH: Kent State University Press
Nichols, John Gough (ed.) (1850), *The Chronicle of Queen Jane, and of Two Years of Queen Mary ... Written by a Resident in the Tower of London*, Camden Society, 48, London: Nichols
Norton Anthology of English Literature (1993), Vol. 1, New York: Norton
Robinson, Hastings (trans.) (1846), *Original Letters relative to the English Reformation*, Cambridge: Cambridge University Press

Stannard, David E. (1977), *The Puritan Way of Death: A Study in Religion, Culture, and Social Change*, New York: Oxford University Press

Travitsky, Betty (ed.) (1981), *Paradise of Women*, Westport, Conn.: Greenwood Press

Warnicke, Retha M. and Bettie Anne Doebler (eds) (1993), Brettergh, Katherine, Harrison, William and William Leigh, in *Deaths Advantage*, New York: Scholars' Facsimiles and Reprints

Warnicke, Retha (1994), 'Eulogies for Women' in Betty S. Travitsky and Adele F. Seeff (eds), *Attending to Women in Early Modern England*, Newark: University of Delaware Press

MARY ELLEN LAMB

The texts by Jane Grey Dudley, are reproduced here, by permission, from the Folger Library copy of the 1570 edition of John Foxe's *Actes and Monumentes* ..., Vol. 2, Bk 10: 1580–85 (*STC* 11223). The text block of the Folger copy is 6¾ in. × 12⅜ in. (p. 1581), including the ruling around it, but not the marginal notes.

The subtitle on the title page to Volume I reads:

The First Volume of the Ecclesiasticall history contaynyng the Actes and Monumentes of thynges passed in euery kynges tyme in this Realme, especially in the Church of England principally to be noted. with a full discourse of such persecutions, horrible troubles, the sufferyng of Martyrs, and other thinges incident, touchyng aswel the sayd Church of England as also Scotland, and all other foreine nations, from the primitiue tyme till the reigne of K Henry viii.

The subtitle on the title page to Volume II reads:

The Second Volume of the Ecclesiastical history, conteynyng the Actes and Monumentes of Martyrs, with a generall discourse of these latter persecutions, horrible troubles, and tumultes, styrred up by the Romish Prelates in the Church, with diuers other thynges incident especially to this Realme of England and Scotland, as partly also to all other foreine nations apparteynyng, from the tyme of K. Henry the viii to Queene Elizabeth our gratious Lady now reygnyng.

On p. 1581, the left-hand marginalia read:

Good workes necessary in a Christian, yet doe they not profite to salvation.
2. Sacramentes.
The Sacrament of Baptisme what it signifieth.
The Sacrament of the Lordes Supper what it signifieth.
What we receiue with the Sacrament.
Rom. 4
Christ had power to turne the bread into his body, is no argument to proue that he dyd so. Fecknam goeth from the word, to the Church.

The top two marginalia on p. 1583 read:

Antichrist also hath hys unitie, which is not to be kept.
The agreement of euill men is no unitie, but a conspiracie.

On p. 1585, the marginalia for Lady Jane read:

February 12
Lady Iane and Lord Gilforde Dudley beheaded.
A wonderful example uppon Morgan the Judge for he gaue sentence agaynst the Lady Iane.
Febru. 21.
Henry Duke of Suffolke beheaded.
L. Thomas Gray apprehended and executed.
Febru. 24.

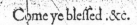

THE FIRST
Volume of the
Ecclesiasticall history contaynyng the Actes and Monumentes
of thynges passed in every kynges tyme
in this Realme, especially in the Church of England principally to be noted, with a full discourse of
such persecutions, horrible troubles, the sufferyng of
Martyrs, and other thynges incident, touchyng aswel
the sayd Church of England as also Scotland,
and all other foreine nations, from the primi-
tive tyme till the reigne of K. Henry viij.

Newly recognised and inlarged
by the Author Iohn Foxe.

AT LONDON
Printed by Iohn Daye, dwellyng
over Aldersgate.

☞ These Bookes are to be sold at his
shop vnder the gate.
1570.
¶Cum gratia & Priuilegio Regiæ Maiestatis.

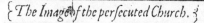

The Image of the persecuted Church.　　The Image of the persecutyng Church.

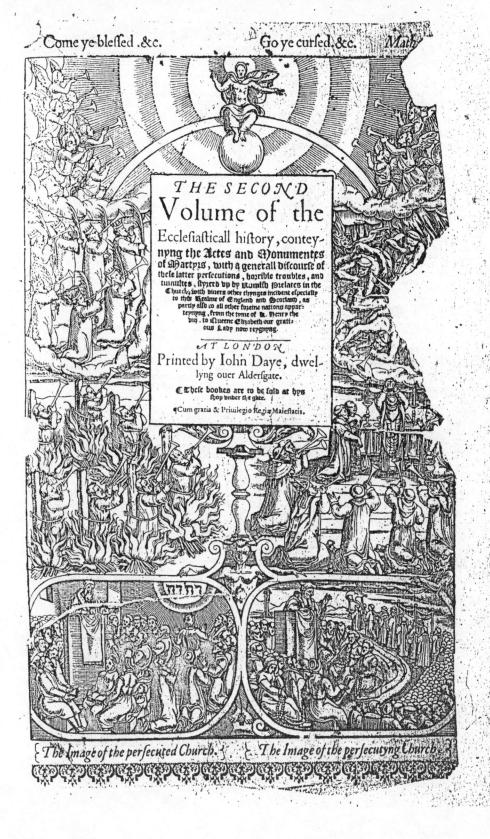

THE SECOND
Volume of the
Ecclesiasticall history, conteynyng the Actes and Monumentes
of Martyrs, with a generall discourse of
these latter persecutions, horrible troubles, and
tumultes, styrred vp by Romish Prelates in the
Church, with diuers other thynges incident especially
to this Realme of England and Scotland, as
partly also to all other foreine nations apper-
teynyng, from the tyme of K. Henry the
viij. to Queene Elizabeth our gracious Lady now reygnyng.

AT LONDON
Printed by Iohn Daye, dwellyng ouer Aldersgate.

These bookes are to be sold at hys
shop vnder the gate.

Cum gratia & Priuilegio Regiæ Maiestatis.

{ The Image of the persecuted Church. }   { The Image of the persecutyng Church }

Q. Mary commeth into the Guild hall. February.1.

Q. Maryes Oration to the Londoners.

Demaundes pretended to be sent from M. Wyat and hys company to Q. Mary.

How he entended the spoile of their goods, it appeareth in that the coming to Southwarke, dyd hurt neyther man, woman, nor chylde, neither in body nor in a penny of their goods.

Q. Mary excuseth her mariage.

The promise of Queene Mary touching her mariage.

In the meane while Sir Peter Carew hearing of that was done, fled into Fraunce, but the other were taki: and Wiat caste towardes London in the beginning of Febuary. The Queene hearing of Wiates cōming, came into the Citie to the Guild hall, where she made a vehement Oration against Wiat: where the contentes, at least the effecte wherof here followeth, as neare as out of her own mouth could be penned.

¶ The Oration of Q. Mary in the Guild Halle.

I Am come vnto you in mine own person, to tell you that which already you see and know: that is, howe traiterously and rebelliously a number of Kentish men haue assembled them selues agaynst both vs and you. Their pretence (as they sayd at the fyrst) was for a mariage determined for vs: to the which, and to all the articles therof ye haue bene made priuy: But sithence we haue raused certain of our priuy Counsail to go again vnto thē, & to demaunde the cause of thys their rebellion: and it appeared then vnto our sayd Counsail, that matter of the mariage seemed to bee but as a Spanish cloke to couer their pretensed purpose against our religiō: So that they arrogantly & traiterously demaūded to haue the gouernaunce of our person, the keeping of the Tower, and the placing of our Counsailers. Now louing subiectes, what I am ye right well know. I am ye owre Queene, to who at my Coronation whē I was wedded to the Realme and lawes of the same (the spousall ring wherof I haue on my finger, which neuer hetherto was, nor hereafter shall be left of you promised your allegeaunce and obedience vnto me. And that I am the right and true inheritour of the Crowne of this Realme of England, I take all Christendome to wytnes. My Father, as ye all knowe, possessed the same regall state, which now rightly is descended vnto me: and to hym alwayes ye shewed your selues most faithfull and louing subiectes, and therefore I doubt not, but ye wil shew your selues likewise to me, and that ye will not suffer a vile Traytor to haue the order and gouernaunce of our person, and to occupy our estate, especially being so vile a Traitor as Wiat is. who most certainly as he hath abused myne ignoraunt Subiectes, which be on his syde, so doth he entend and purpose the destruction of you, and spoyle of your goodes. And this I say to you in the word of a Prince: I can not tell how naturally the Mother loueth the Childe, for I was neuer the mother of any, but certainly, if a Prince and Gouernour may as naturally & earnestly loue her Subiectes as the Mother doth the Child, then assure your selues, that I being your Lady and Maistres, doe as earnestly and as tenderly loue and fauour you. And I thus louing you, can not but thinke that ye do hartely and faythfully loue me: & then I doubt not, but we shall geue these rebels a short and speedy ouerthrow.

As concerning the mariage, ye shall vnderstand that I enterprised not the doing therof without aduise, and that by the aduise of all our priuy Counsail: who so considered and weyed the great commodities that might ensue therof, that they not onely thought it very honorable, but also expedient, both for the wealth of our realme, and also of all you our Subiectes. And as touching my selfe, I assure you, I am not so bent to my will, neither so precise nor affectionate, that either for myne own pleasure I would chuse where I last, or that I am so desirous as needes I would haue one. For God I thanke hym, to whom be the prayse therefore, I haue hetherto lyued a Virgin, and doubt nothing, but wyth Gods grace am able so to liue still. But if, as my Progenitours haue done before, it might please God that I might leaue some truite of my body behinde me to be your Gouernour, I trust ye would not onely reioyce therat, but also I know it would bee to your great comfort. And certainly, if I eyther did thinke or know that this mariage were to the hurt of any of you my Commons, or to the empechment of any part or parcell of the royall state of this realme of England: I woulde neuer consent thereunto, neyther would I euer marry whyle I lyued. And in the worde of a Queene I promise you, that if it shall not probably appeare to all the Nobility and Commons in the hygh Court of Parlament, that this mariage shalbe for the high benefite and commodity of all the whole Realme, then I wyll abstayne from mariage whyle I lyue.

And now good Subiectes, plucke vp your harts, and like true mē, stand fast against these rebels, both our enemies and yours, and feare them not: for I assure you, I feare them nothing at all, and I wyll leaue wyth you

my Lord Haward & my Lord Treasurer, who shalbe assistentes wyth the Maior for your defence.

¶ Here is to be noted, that at the comming of Q. Mary to the Guild Hall, being bruted before that she was cōming with harnessed men: such a feare came among thē, that a number of the Londoners fearing lest they should bee there entrapped and put to death, made out of the gate before her entring in. Furthermore, note that when she had ended her Oration (which she seemed to haue perfectly conned without booke) Winchester standing by her, when the Oration was done, with great admiration cried to the people: O how happy are we, to who God hath geuē such a wise & learned Prince? &c.

Two dayes after, which was ye iii. of February, the Lord Cobham was committed to the Tower, & M.Wiat entred into Southwarke. Who, for somuch as he could not enter that way into London, returning an other way by Kingstone with his army, came vp through the streetes to Ludgate, & returning thece, he was resisted at Temple barre, & there retoled hym selfe to ye: Clement Parson, and so was brought by hym to ye Court, & with hym the residue of hys armie (for before, ye: George Harpar & almost halfe of his men ranne away frō hym at Kingstone bridge) were also taken, & about an hondreth killed, and they that were taken were had to prison, & a great many of thē were hāged: & he hym self afterward executed at ye Tower hill, & then quartered. Whose head after being set vp vpō Hay hill, was there stollen away, & great search made for ye same. Of which story ye shall heare more (the Lord willing) hereafter.

The xii. day of February was beheaded the Lady Iane, to whom was sent maister Fecknam, alias Howman, from the Queene two dayes before her death, to cōmine with her, and to reduce her from the doctrine of Christ, to Q. Maries religion. The effecte of which communication here followeth.

¶ The communication had betwene the Lady IANE and FECKNAM.

Fecknam. Madame, I lament your heauy case, and yet I doubt not, but that you beare out this sorowe of yours wyth a constant and pacient mynde.

Iane. You are welcome vnto me Syr, if your coming be to geue Christian exhortation. And as for my heauy case (I thanke God) I do so litle lament it, that rather I accompt the same for a more manifest declaration of gods fauour toward me, the euer he shewed me at any tyme before: And therefore there is no cause why either you, or other which beare me good wyll, should lament or be grieued wyth this my case, being a thing so profitable for my soule health.

Feck. I am here come to you at this present sent from the Queene and her Counsayle, to instruct you in the true doctrine of the right fayth: although I haue so great confidence in you, that I shall haue (I trust) litle nede to trauail wyth you much therein.

Iane. Forsooth I hartely thāke the Queenes highnes, which is not vnmindfull of her hūble subiect: & I hope likewise that you no lesse will do your dutie therin both truly & faithfully, according to that you were sent for.

Feck. What is then required of a Christian?

Iane. That he should beleue in God, the father, the sonne, and the holy Ghost, three persons and one God.

Feck. Whate is there nothing els to bee required or looked for in a Christian, but to beleue in hym?

Iane. Yes, we must also loue hym with all our hart, with all our soule, and wyth all our mynd, and our neyghbour as our selfe.

Feck. Why then fayth iustifieth not, nor saueth not.

Iane. Yes verely, fayth (as Paul sayth) only iustifieth.

Feck. Why sayth Paule sayth: If I haue all faith without loue, it is nothing.

Iane. True it is: for how can I loue hym, whom I trust not: or how can I trust him whom I loue not? Fayth and loue goeth both together, and yet loue is cōprehended in fayth.

Fecknam.

I Iohn.3.

M.Wyat in Southwarke.

M.Wyat came to Ludgate.

M.Wyat apprehended at Temple barre.

M.Wyat executed.

February 14.

Talke betwene the Lady Iane and Fecknam.

Lady Iane cōstantly & godly taketh her trouble.

Fayth onely iustifieth.

Feck. How shall we loue our neighbour?

Iane. To loue our neighbour, is to fæde the hungry, to cloath the naked, and geue drinke to the thirsty, and to do to him, as we would do to our selues.

Feck. Whē then it is necessary vnto saluation to doo good workes also, & it is not sufficient onely to beleue.

Iane. I deny that, and I affirme that fayth onely saueth: but it is mæte for a Christian, in somuch that hee followeth hys maister Christ, to do good workes: yet may we not say that they profit to saluation. For when we haue done all, yet we be vnprofitable seruauntes, and fayth onely in Christes bloud saueth vs.

Feck. How many Sacraments are there?

Iane. Two. The one the sacramēt of Baptisme, and the other the sacrament of the Lordes supper.

Fecknam. No, there are seuen.

Iane. By what scripture finde you that?

Feck. Wel, we wil talke of that hereafter. But what is signified by your two sacramentes?

Iane. By the sacrament of Baptisme I am washed with water, and regenerated by the spirite, and that washing is a token to mē that I am the childe of God. The sacrament of the Lords supper offred vnto me, is a sure seale and testimonie that I am by the bloud of Christ, whych he shed for me on the crosse, made partaker of the euerlasting kingdome.

Feck. Why? what do you receiue in that sacrament? Do you not receyue the very body & bloud of Christ?

Iane. No surely, I do not so beleue. I thynke that at þe supper I neither receiue flesh nor bloud, but bread and wyne: Which bread when it is broken, and the wyne when it is dronken, putteth me in remembraunce how that for my synnes the body of Christ was broken, and hys bloud shed on the crosse, and with that bread and wine I receiue the benefites that come by the breaking of his body and sheding of hys bloude for our sinnes on the crosse.

Feck. Why? doth not Christ speake these wordes: Take, eate, this is my body? Require you any playner wordes? doth he not say it is hys body?

Iane. I graunt he sayth so: and so he sayth, I am the vine, I am the doore, but he is neuer the more for that the doore nor the vine. Doth not Saint Paule say, he calleth thinges that are not, as though they were? God forbyd that I should say that I eate the very naturall body and bloude of Christ: for then eyther I should plucke away my redemption, either els there were two bodies, or two Christes. One body was tormented on the crosse. And if they did eate an other body, then had he two bodies: eyther els if hys body were eaten, then was it not broken vpon the crosse: or if it were broken vpon the crosse, it was not eaten of hys disciples.

Feck. Why? is it not as possible that Christ by hys power could make hys body both to be eaten and broken, as to be borne of a woman without sæde of man, and as to walke vpon the sea hauing a body, and other such like miracles as he wrought by his power onely?

Iane. Yes verely: if God would haue done at his supper any miracle, he might haue done so: but I say that then hee minded no worke nor miracle, but onely to breake his body, and shed his bloud on the crosse for our sinnes. But I pray you aunswere me to this one question: where was Christ when he sayd: Take, eate, this is my body? Was he not at the table when hee sayd so? He was at that tyme aliue, and suffred not tyll the next day. What tooke he but bread? What brake he but bread? and what gaue he but bread? Looke what he tooke, he brake: and looke what he brake, he gaue: and looke what he gaue, they did eate: and yet all this while he him selfe was alyue, and at supper before hys Disciples, or els they were deceiued.

Feck. You ground your faith vpon such authours as say and vnsay both wyth a breath, and not vpon the Church, to whom ye ought to geue credite.

Iane. No, I ground my fayth on Gods worde, and not vpon the church. For if the church be a good church, the fayth of the church must be tried by Gods worde, and not Gods worde by the Church, neyther yet my fayth. Shall I beleue the Church because of antiquitie? or shall I geue credite to the Church that taketh away from me the halfe parte of the Lordes Supper, and wyll not let any lay mā receiue it in both kindes? Whych thing if they deny to be, then deny they to be part of our saluation. And I say that is an euyll church, and not the Spouse of Christ; but the Spouse of the Deuill that altereth the Lordes supper, and both taketh from it, & addeth to it. To that church (say I) God wyll adde plages, and from that Church wyll he take their part out of the booke of lyfe. Doo they learne that of S. Paule, when he ministred to the Corinthians in both kyndes? Shall I beleue thys Church? God forbid.

Feck. That was done for a good intent of the church, to auoyd an heresy that sprong on it.

Iane. Why? shall the Church alter Gods wyll and ordinaunce for a good intent? How did king Saul? The Lord God defend.

With these and such lyke persuasions hee woulde haue had her leaue to the Church, but it woulde not be. There were many moe thinges whereof they reasoned, but these were the chiefest.

After thys Fecknam tooke hys leaue, saying that he was sory for her: For I am sure (quoth he) that we two shall neuer mæte.

Iane. True it is (sayd she) that we shall neuer mæte, except God turne your hart. For I am assured, vnlesse you repent and turne to God, you are in an euill case: & I pray God, in þe bowels of his mercy, to send you his holy spirit: for he hath geuen you his great gift of vtterance, if it pleased him also to open þe eyes of your hart.

¶ A letter of the Lady Iane sent vnto her Father.

Father, although it hath pleased God to hasten my death by you, by whom my lyfe should rather haue bene lengthened: yet can I so paciētly take it, as I yeld God more harty thākes for shortening my wofull dayes, then if all the worlde had bene geuen into my possession with lyfe lengthened at my owne will. And albeit I am well assured of your impacient dolours, redoubled manyfolde waies, both in bewayling your owne woe, and especially (as I heare) my infortunate state: yet my deare father (if I may without offence reioyce in my owne mishaps) me seemes in this I may account my selfe blessed, that washing my handes with the innocencie of my fact, my giltles bloud may cry before the Lorde, mercy, mercye to the innocent. And yet though I must nedes acknowledge, that being constrained, and, as you wot wel inough, continually assayed, in takīg vpon me I seemed to consent, & therin greuously offēded, yet the Quéene and her lawes: yet doe I assuredly trust that this myne offence towardes God is so much the lesse, in that being in so royall estate as I was, mine enforced honour neuer agreed with mine innocent hart. And thus good father I haue opened vnto you the state wherin I presētly stand, whose death at hand, although to you perhaps it may seeme right wofull, to me there is nothing that can bee more welcome then from this vale of miserye to aspyre to that heauēly throne of all ioy and pleasure with Christ our Sauiour. In whose stedfast fayth (if it may be lawfull for the daughter to so wryte to the Father) the Lord that hitherto hath strengthened you, so cōtinue you that at the last we may meete in heauen with the Father, the Sonne, and the holy Ghost.

At what time her father was flourishing in freedome and prosperitie in the time of King Edward, there belonged vnto him a certeyne learned mā, studēt and Graduate of the Vniuersity of Oxford. Who then being Chaplaine to the sayd Duke, and a sincere Preacher (as hee appeared) of the Gospell, according to the doctrine of that time sette forth and receiued, shortly after that the state of religion began to alter by Quéene Mary, altered also in hys profession wyth the tyme,

III.iij.

time, and of a Protestant became a friende and defender of the Popes proceedinges. At whose sodaine mutation and inconstant mutabilitie, this Christian Lady being not a lyttle agreued, and most of all lamenting the daungerous state of hys soule in Hyding so away for feare, from the way of truth, writeth her mynde vnto him in a sharpe and vehemēt letter: which as it appeareth to proceede of an earnest & zealous hart, so would God it might take such effecte with him, as to reduce him to repentance, & to take better hold agayn for the health and wealth of hys own soule. The coppe of the letter is this as followeth.

¶An other Letter of the Lady Iane to *M. H.* late Chaplayne to the Duke of Suffolke her father, and then fallen from the truth of Gods most holy worde.

SO oft as I call to mind the dreadfull and fearefull saying of God : *That he which layeth hold vpō the plough and looketh backe, is not meete for the kingdome of heauen:* and on the other side, the cōfortable wordes of our Sauiour Christ to all those that forsaking them selues, do folow hym: I can not but meruell at thee and lamēt thy case: which semedst sometyme to be y liuely mēber of Christ, but now the desponed impe of the deuill, some tyme the beutifull temple of God, but now the stinking and filthy kennell of Sathan, sometyme the vnspotted spouse of Christ , but now the vnshamefast paramour of Antichrist, sometyme my faithfull brother, but now a straunger, and Apostata, sometyme a stout Christen souldier, but now a cowardly runcaway, yea, when I consider these thinges, I can not but speake to thee, and crie out vpon thee , thou seede of Sathan, and not of Iuda, whom the deuill hath deceiued, the world hath beguiled, and the desire of life subuerted, and made thee of a Christian an Infidell : wherfore hast thou taken the Testamēt of the Lord in thy mouth? wherfore hast thou preached y law and the will of God to others? wherfore hast thou instructed other to be strong in Christ, whē thou thy selfe doest now so shamefully shrinke , and so horribly abuse the Testament & law of the Lord? when thou thy selfe preachest, not to steale, yet most abhominably stealest , not from men but from God, & committyng most heinous sacrilege, robbest Christ thy Lord of his right mēbers thy body and thy soule , and chosest rather to lyue miserably with shame

to the world, then to dye and gloriously with honour to reigne with Christ, in whom euen in death is lyfe? why doest thou now shew thy self most weake, when in deede thou oughtest to be most stronge? The strength of a forte is not knowen before the assault : but thou yeldest thy holde before any battrie be made.

Oh wretched and vnhappy man, what art thou but dust and ashes? & wilt thou resist thy maker that fashioned thee and framed thee? wilt thou now forsake hym that called thee from the custome gatheryng among the Romish Antichristians, to be an Ambassadour and messenger of his eternall worde? He that first framed thee, and since thy first creation and birth preserued thee, nourished and kept thee, yea and inspired thee with the spirite of knowledge (I can not say of grace) shall he not now possesse thee? Darest thou deliuer vp thy selfe to an other, being not thine own but his? How canst thou hauyng knowledge , or how darest thou neglect the law of of the Lord, and folow the vayne traditions of men: and where as thou hast bene a publicke professour of his name, become now a defacer of his glory? wilt thou refuse the true God, and worshyp the inuention of mā, the golden calfe, the whore of Babylon, the Romish Religion, the abominable Idol the most wicked Masse? wilt thou torment agayne , rent, and teare the most pretious body of our Sauiour Christ with thy bodily and fleshly teeth? wilt thou take vppon thee to offer vp any Sacrifice vnto God for our sinnes, cōsidering that Christ offered vp him self (as Paul saith) vpon y Crosse a liuely sacrifice once for all? Canst neither y punishmēt of the Israelites (which for their Idolatry they so oft receaued) nor y terrible threatnynges of the Prophetes, nor the curses of Gods owne mouth feare thee to honour any other God then hym? Doest thou so regard him that spared not his deare and onely sonne for thee, so diminishyng, yea, vtterly extin-

guishyng his glory that thou wilt attribute the prayse and honour due vnto him to the Idoles, which haue mouthes and speake not, eyes and see not, eares & heare not : which shalt perish with them that made them?

What sayth the Prophet Baruch, where he reciteth the Epistle of Ieremy written to the captiue Iewes? Did he not forewarne them that in Babylō they should see Gods of gold, siluer, wood, and stone borne vpon mens shoulders, to cast a feare before the heathen: But be not ye afrayd of them (sayth Ieremy) nor do as other do : But whēn you see other worship them (say you in your hartes: it is thou(O Lord)that oughtest onely to be worshipped: for as for those Gods, the Carpenter framed them and polished them, yea , gilded be they, and layd ouer with siluer and vayne things: and cānot speake. He sheweth more ouer, the abuse of their deckings, how the Priestes tooke of their ornamentes and apparelled their women withall : how one holdeth a scepter , an other a swoord in his hand, and yet can they iudge in no matter, nor defend them selues , much lesse any other, from either battell or murther, nor yet from gnawyng of wormes, nor any other euill thyng. These, and such lyke wordes, speaketh Ieremy vnto thē, wherby he prouch the to be but vayne thinges, & no Gods. And at last he concludeth thus: Confounded be they that worship them. They were warned by Ieremy, and thou as Ieremy hast warned other, and art warned thy selfe by many Scriptures in many places. God sayth: he is a ielous God , which will haue all honour, glory, and worship geuen to him onely. And Christ sayth in the fourth of Luke to Sathan which tempted him: euen to the same Sathan, the same Belzebub, the same deuill, which hath preuailed agaynst thee: It is writtē (sayth he) thou shalt honour the Lorde thy God, and him onely shalt thou serue.

These and such like do prohibite thee and all Christians to worship any other God then which was before all worldes, and layd the foundations both of heauen and earth: and wilt thou honour a detestable Idol, inuented by Romish Popes, & the abominable Colledge of craftie Cardinals? Christ offered himselfe vp once for all, & wylt thou offer him vp again daily at thy pleasure? But thou wylt say, thou doest it for a good intent. O sinke of sinne: Oh childe of perdition: doest thou breame therein of a good euent , where thy conscience beareth the wytnes of Gods threatned wrath against thee? How did Saule, who for that he disobeyed the word of the lord for a good intent, was throwen from his worldly and temporall kingdome. Shalt thou then that doest deface Gods honor and robbe him of hys right, enherite the eternall and heauenly kingdome? wilt thou for a good intent dishonour God, offende thy brother, and daunger thy soule, wherefore Christ hath shedde hys most precious bloud? wilt thou for a good intent plucke Christ out of heauen, and make his death voyde, and deface the triumph of his crosse by offering hym vp dayly? work thou either for feare of death, or hope of lyfe, denye and refuse thy God, who enriched thy pouertie, healed thy infirmitie, & helped thee to thy victory, if thou couldest haue kept it: Doest thou not cōsider that the threed of thy lyfe hāgeth vpon him that made thee, who can (as his will is) eyther twine it harder to last the longer, or vntwine it agayne to breake it the sooner? Doest thou not then remember the saying of Dauid a notable king, to teach thee a miserable wretch, in his 104. Psalme, where hee sayth thus: VVhen thou takest away thy spirite (oh Lord) from men, they die and are turned agayne to their dust : but whē thou lettest thy breath go forth, they shall be made, and thou shalt renne the face of the earth. Remember the saying of Christ in his Gospell. VVhosoeuer seeketh to saue hys lyfe , shall lose it : but who soeuer will lose hys lyfe for my sake, shall finde it . And in the same place: VVhosoeuer loueth father or mother aboue me , is not meete for me . He that will follow me , let him forsake him selfe and take vp his crosse and follow me , what crosse? the crosse of infamie and shame, of miserye and pouertye, of affliction and persecution for his names sake . Let the oft falling of those heauenly showers pearce thy stony hart . Let the two edged swoord of Gods holy worde shere asunder the sinowes of worldly respectes euen to the very marrowe of thy carnall hart , that thou mayest once againe forsake thy selfe and embrace Christ . And like as good subiectes wyll not refuse to hasard all in the defence of their earthly and temporall Gouernour, so sit not like a white liuered milkesop frō the standing where in thy chief captaine Christ hath set thee in array of thys life . Viriliter age , confortetur cor tuum , sustine dominum. Fight māfully, come life, come death: y quarel is Gods, and vndoubtedly the victory is ours.

But

But thou wilt say, I will not breake vnitie. what? not the vnitie of Sathan and his members? not the vnitie of darkenes, the agreement of Antichrist and hys adherentes? May thou because thy selfe with the fonde imagination of such a vnitie as is among the enemies of Christ. were not the false Prophetes in an vnitie? were not Iosephes brethren and Iacobs sonnes in an vnitie? were not the Heathen, as the Amelechites, the Pheresites and Iebusites in an vnitie? were not the Scribes and Pharisies in an vnitie? Doth not king Dauid testifie: *Conuenerunt in vnum aduersus dominum?* yea theues, murtherers, conspiratours haue their vnitie. But what vnitie? Tully sayd of amitie: *Amicitia non est, nisi inter bonos.* But marke my friend, yea friend, if thou be not Gods enemy: there is no vnitie but where Christ knitteth the knot among such as be his. Yea, be wel assured, that where his truth is resident, there it is verified that he him selfe sayth: *Non veni mittere pacem in terram, sed gladium.* &c. but to set one against an other, the sonne against the father, and the daughter against the mother in law. Because not thy selfe therfore with the glittring and glorious name of vnitie: for Antichrist hath this vnitie, not yet in deede, but in name. The agreement of ill men is not an vnitie, but a conspiracie.

Thou hast heard some threatninges, some curses, and some admonitions out of the scripture to those that loue them selues aboue Christ. Thou hast heard also the sharpe and biting wordes to those that denye him for loue of lyfe. Sayth he not: *He that denieth me before men, I wyll deny him before my father in heauen?* And to the same effect writeth Paule, *Hebr. vj. It is impossible* (sayth he) *that they which were once lightned, & haue tasted of the heauenly gift, and were partakers of the holy Ghost, and haue tasted of the good worde of God, if they fall and slide away, crucifying to them selues the Sonne of God afreshe, and making of hym a mocking stocke, shoulde bee renued againe by repentaunce.* And a=gayne sayth he: *if wee shall willingly sinne after wee haue receiued the knowledge of his truth, there is no oblation left for sinne, but the terrible expectation of iudgement and fire, which shall deuour the aduersaries.* Thus S. Paule writeth, and this thou readest, and doest thou not quake and tremble?

Well, if these terrible & thundring threatninges can not stirre thee to cleaue vnto Christ, & forsake the world: yet let the sweete consolations & promises of the Scriptures, let the example of Christ and his Apostles, holy Martyrs and Confessours encourage thee to take faster hold by Christ. Harken what hee sayth: *Blessed are you when men reuile you, and persecute you for my sake & reioyce and be glad, for great is your reward in heauen: for so persecuted they the Prophetes that were before you.* Heare what Esay the Prophet sayth: *Feare not the curse of men, be not afrayde of their blasphemies and reuilinges: for Wormes and mothes shall eate them vp like cloth and wool, but my righteousnes shall endure for euer, and my sauing health from generation to generation. What art thou then* (sayth he) *that fearest a mortall man, the childe of man, which fadeth away like the flower: and forgettest the Lord that made thee, that spread out the heauens, and layd the foundation of the earth? I am thy Lord thy God, that make the sea to rage and be styll, whose name is the Lord of hostes. I shall put my word in thy mouth and defend thee with the turning of an hand.* And our Sauiour Christ sayeth to his disciples: *They shall accuse you and bring you before Princes and Rulers for my names sake, and some of you they shall persecute and kill: but feare you not* (sayth he) *nor care you not what you shall say: for it is the spirite of your father that speaketh within you. Euen the very heares of your head are all numbred. Lay vp treasure for your selues* (sayth he) *where no theefe commeth, nor moth corrupteth. Feare not them that kill the body but are not able to kill the soule, but feare hym that hath power to destroy both soule and body. If ye were of the worlde, the worlde would loue hys owne: but because ye are not of the worlde, but I haue chosen you out of the worlde, therefore the worlde hateth you.*

Let these and such like consolations taken out of the scriptures, strengthen you to Godward. Let not the examples of holy men and women go out of your minde, as Daniell and the rest of the Prophetes: of the three Children, of Eleazarus that constant father, of the vij. of the Machabeies children, of Peter, Paule, Steuen, and other Apostles and holy Martyrs in the beginning of the church: As of good Simeon Archbishop of Seloma, and Zetrophone, with infinite other vnder Saporesthe King of the Persians and Indians, who contemned all tormentes deuysed by the tyrauntes, for their Sauiours sake. Returne, returne againe into Christes warre, and as becommeth a faithfull warriour, put on that armour that

---

S. Paule teacheth to be most necessary for a Christian man. And aboue all thinges take to you the shield of fayth, and be you prouoked by Christes own example to withstand the deuill, to forsake the world, and to become a true and faithfull member of his misticall body, who spared not his owne body for our sinnes.

Throwe downe your selfe with the feare of his threatned vengeaunce for this so great & haynous an offence of Apostasie: and comfort your selfe on ye other part with the mercy, bloud & promise of him that is ready to turne vnto you when soeuer you turne vnto him. Disdayne not to come agayne with the lost sonne, seing you haue so wandred with him. Be not ashamed to turne agayne with him from the swyll of straungers, to the delicates of your most benigne & louing father, acknowledging that you haue sinned against heauen & earth. Against heauen by staying the glorious name of God, and causing his most sincere and pure word to be euill spoken of through you. Against earth by offending so many of your weake brethren, to whom you haue bene a stumbling blocke through your sodayne slyding. Be not abashed to come home agayne with Mary, and weepe bitterly with Peter, not onely with shedding the teares of your bodily eyes, but also powring out the streames of your hart, to wash away out of the sight of God, the filth and myre of your offensiue fal. Be not abashed to say with the publicane, *Lord be mercifull vnto me a sinner.* Remember the horrible hystory of Iulian of olde, and the lamentable case of Spira of late, whose case (me thinke) should be yet so greene in your remembraunce, that being a thing of our tyme, you should feare the lyke inconuenience seyng you are fallen into the lyke offence.

Last of all, let the liuely remembraunce of the last day be alwayes afore your eyes, remembring the terrour that such shall be in at that tyme, with the runnagates and fugitiues from Christ, which seeing woe by the world then by heauen, more by their life then by him that gaue them lyfe, did thinke, yea did cleare fall away from him that forsoke not them: and contrary wise the inestimable ioyes prepared for them that fearing no perill nor breaking death, haue manfully fought, and victoriously triumphed ouer all power of darkenes, ouer hell, death, and damnation, though their most redoubted captaine Christ, who nowe stretcheth out his armes to receaue you, ready to fall vpon your necke and kisse you, and last of all to feast you with the deinties and delicates of hys own precious bloud, which vndoubtedly, if it might stand with his determinate purpose, he would not let to shed agayne, rather then you should be loste. To whom with the father & the holy ghost be all honour, prayse and glory euerlastingly. Amen.

Be constant, be constant, feare not for payne,
Christ hath redeemed thee, and heauen is thy gayne.

¶ A Letter written by the Lady Iane in the ende of the new Testament in Greeke, the which she sent vnto her Sister Lady Katherine, the nyght before she suffered.

I Haue here sent you (good sister Katherine) a booke, which although it be not outwardly trimmed with gold, yet inwardly it is more worth the precious stones. It is the booke (deare Sister) of the law of the Lord. It is his Testament & last wil which he bequethed vnto vs wretches: which shal lead you to the path of eternall ioy: and if you with a good mind read it, and with an earnest minde to purpose to folow it, it shall bryng you to an immortall & euerlasting life. It shall teach you to liue, and learne you to dye. It shall wynne you more the you should haue gayned by the possession of your wofull fathers landes. For, as if God had prospered him you should haue inherited his landes: so if you apply diligently this booke, seekyng to direct your life after it, you shalbe an inheritour of such riches, as neither the couetous shall withdraw from you, neither theefe shall steale, neither yet the mother corrupt. Desire with Dauid (good Sister) to vnderstand the law of the Lord your God. Lyue still to dye, that you (by death) may purchase eternall life. And trust not that the tendernes of your age shall lengthen your life. For, as soone (if God call) goeth the younge as the olde, and labour alwayes to learne to die. Desire the world, deny the deuill, and despise the flesh, and delite your selfe onely in the Lord. Be penitent for your sinnes, and yet dispayre not: be strong in fayth, and yet presume not, & desire with S. Paul to be dissolued & to bee with Christ, with whom euen in death there is life. Be like the good

J.J.Jt.iii. ser=

A letter full of exhortation of the Lady Iane to the Lady Katherine her sister, to read Gods worde.

So liue to die, that by death you may liue.

Math.10.
Heb.6.
Rom.10.
Math.5.
Esay.51.
Math.10.
Luke.12.
Math.10.
Iohn.15.

seruaunt, and euen at midnight be waking, lest when death comneth and stealeth vpon you like a theefe in the night, you be with the euill seruaunt found sleeping, and lest for lacke of oyle, you be told like the fiue foolish women: and like him that had not on the wedding garmēt, and then ye be cast out from the mariage. Reioyce in Christ, as I doe. Followe the steppes of your Master Christ, and take vp your Crosse: lay your sinnes on his backe and alwayes embrace him. And as touchyng my death, reioyce as I do (good Sister) that I shalbe deliuered of this corruption, and put on incorruption. For I am assured that I shall for losing of a mortall life, winne an immortal life: the which I pray God graunt you, and send you of his grace to lyue in his feare, and to dye in the true Christian faith, from the which (in Gods name) I exhort you that you neuer swarue, neither for hope of life, nor for feare of death. For if ye will deny his truth to lengthen your life, God will deny you, and yet shorten your dayes. And if you will cleaue vnto him, he will prolong your dayes to your comfort and his glory: to the which glory God bryng me now, and you hereafter when it pleaseth him to call you. Fare you well good Sister, and put your onely trust in God, who onely must helpe you.

A prayer of the Lady Iane.

Here foloweth a certayne effectuall prayer made by the Lady Iane, in the time of her trouble.

O Lord, thou God and father of my life, heare me poore & desolate womā, which flyeth vnto thee, only in all troubles and miseries. Thou O Lord art the onely defendour and deliuerer of those that put there trust in thee: and therfore I beyng defiled with sinne, encombred with afflictiō, vnquieted with troubles, wrapped in cares, ouerwhelmed with miseries, vexed with tēptations, and greuously tormented with the long imprisonment of this vyle Masse of clay my sinfull body: do come vnto thee (O mercifull Sauiour) crauyng thy mercy and helpe without the which so litle hope of deliueraunce is left, that I may vtterly despayre of any libertie. Albeit it is expedient, that seyng our lyfe standeth vpon trying, we should be visited sometyme with some aduersity, wherby we might both be tried whether we be of thy flocke or no, & also know thee & our selues the better: yet thou that saydest that thou wouldest not suffer vs to be tempted aboue our power, be mercifull vnto me now a miserable wretch, I beseech thee: which with Salomon doe cry vnto thee, humbly desiryng thee, that I may neither be to much puffed vp with prosperity, neither to much pressed downe with aduersitie: lest I beyng to full, shoulde deny thee my God, or beyng to low brought should despayre and blaspheme thee my Lord and Sauiour. O mercyfull God, consider my misery best knowē vnto thee, & be thou now vnto me a strong tower of defence, I hūbly require thee. Suffer me not to be tempted aboue my power, but either be thou a deliuerer vnto me out of this great miserie, either els geue me grace patiently to beare thy heauy hand and sharpe correction. It was thy right hand that deliuered the people of Israell out of the handes of Pharao, which for the space of iiij. C. yeares did oppresse them and keepe them in bondage. Let it therfore likewise seeme good to thy fatherly goodnes to deliuer me sorowfull wretch (for whom thy sonne Christ shed his precious bloud on the Crosse) out of this miserable captiuitie and bondage, wherein I am now. How long wilt thou be absent? for euer? Oh Lord hast thou forgotten to be gracious, and hast thou shut vp thy louyng kyndnes in displeasure? wilt thou be no more entreated? Is thy mercy cleane gone for euer, and thy promise come vtterly to an ende for euermore? why doest thou make so long taryng? shall I despayre of thy mercy O God? farre be that from me. I am thy workemanshyp created in Christ Iesu: giue me grace therfore to tary thy leasure, and patiently to beare thy workes: assuredly knowyng, that as thou canst, so thou wilt deliuer me when it shall please thee, nothyng doubtyng or mystrustyng thy goodnes towardes me: for thou wottest better what is good for me then I do: Therfore do with me in all things what thou wilt: and plage me what way thou wilt. Onely in the meane tyme arme me I beseech thee, with thy armour, that I may stād fast, my loynes beyng gyrded about with veritie, hauyng on the brest plate of ryghteousnes, and shod with the shoes prepared by the Gospell of peace, aboue all thynges takyng to me the shield of fayth, wherewith I may bee able to quench all the fiery dartes of the wicked, and takyng the helmet of saluation and the sword of the spirite, which is thy most holy word; prayng alwaies with al maner of prayer & supplicatiō, that I may referre my selfe wholy to thy will, abidyng thy pleasure and comfortyng my selfe in those troubles that it shall

Psal.77.

Ephes.6.

please thee to send me: seyng such troubles be profitable for me, and seyng I am assuredly persuaded that it can not bee but well, all that thou doest. Heare me O mercifull father for his sake, whom thou wouldest should be a sacrifice for my sinnes: to whom with thee and the holy Ghost be all honour and glory. Amen.

After these thyngs thus declared, it remaineth now, commyng to the end of this vertuous Lady, next to inferre the maner of her execution, with the wordes and behauiour of her in tyme of her death.

These are the wordes that the Lady Iane spake vpon the scaffolde at the houre of her death.

First when she mounted vpon the Scaffold, she sayd to the people standyng there about: good people I am come hether to dye, and by a law I am condemned to the same. The fact agaynst the Queenes highnes was vnlawfull, and the consenting therunto by me: but touchyng the procurement and desire thereof by me as on my behalfe, I do wash my handes therof in innocency before God, and the face of you, good Christian people, this day: and therwith she wrong her handes, wherein she had her booke. Then sayd she, I pray you all, good Christian people, to beare me witnes that I dye a true Christian woman, and that I do looke to be saued by no other meane, but onely by the mercy of God in the bloud of his onely sonne Iesus Christ: and I confesse that when I did know the word of God, I neglected the same, loued my selfe and the world, and therfore this plage and punishment is happily and worthely happened vnto me for my sinnes: and yet I thanke God of his godnes that he hath thus giuen me a tyme and respite to repēt: and now (good people) while I am alyue I pray you assiste me with your prayers. And thē kneling downe she turned her to Feckham sayng: shall I say this Psalme: and she sayd, yea. Then sayd she the Psalme of Miserere mei Deus in English: in most deuonte maner throughout to the ēd: & then she stode vp and gaue her maydē Maistres Ellyn her gloues and handkercheffe, and her booke to Maister Bruges, and then she vntied her gowne, and the hangman pressed vpon her to helpe her of with it, but she desyryng hym to let her alone, turned towardes her two Gentlewomen who helped her of therewith, and also with her frowes past and neckerchefe, giuyng to her a fayre handkerchefe to knyt about her eyes. Then the hangman kneeled downe and asked her forgeuenes, whom she forgaue most willyngly. Then he willed her to stand vpon the straw: which doing she saw the blocke. Then she sayd, I pray you dispatch me quickly. Then she kneeled downe, saying: will you take it of before I lay me downe: and the hangman sayd, no Madame. Thē tyed she ȝ kerchefe about her eyes, and feelyng for ȝ blocke, she sayd, what shall I do: where is it: where is it: Þ One of the standers by guidyng her thereunto, she layd her head downe vpon the blocke, and then stretched forth her body and sayd: Lord into thy handes I commend my spirite, and so finished her lyfe in the yeare of our Lord God. 1553. the 12. day of February.

Certayne prety verses wrytten by the sayd Lady Iane wyth a pynne.

Non aliena putes homini quæ obtingere possunt,
Sors hodierna mihi, tunc erit illa tibi.

Iane Dudley.

Deo iuuante, nil nocet liuor malus:
Et non iuuante, nil iuuat labor grauis.

Post tenebras spero lucem.

Certayne Epitaphes wrytten in commendation of the worthy Lady Iane Gray.

De Iana Graia Ioan. Parkhurst Carmen.

Miraris Ianam Graio sermone valere?
Quo primum nata est tempore, Graia fuit.

In

The wordes and behauiour of the Lady Iane vpon the scaffolde.

The second confession & faythe of the Lady Iane.

Graia being her surname signifieth in Latin a Grecian.

The Constancy and Fortitude of this Lady Jane at the Death in 1554 Grau...de...in 1775. first 221.

in hiſtoriam Iana. I. F.

Tu, quibus iſta legas incertum eſt lector, ocellis:
Ipſe equidem ſiccis ſcribere non potui.

De Iana, D. Laurenty Humfredi decaſtichon.

Iana iacet ſævo non æquæ vulnere mortis,
Nobilis ingenio, ſanguine, martyrio.
Ingenium latijs ornauit fœmina muſis,
Fœmina virgineo tota dicata choro.
Sanguine clara fuit, regali ſtirpe creata,
Ipſaq; Reginæ nobilitata throno.
Bis Gratia eſt, pulchrè Graijs nutrita camænis,
Et priſco Graium ſanguine creta ducum.
Bis Martyr, ſacræ fidei veriſſima teſtis:
Atque vacans regni crimine, Iana iacet.

1554.
February.

Thus the xii.day of February (as I ſayd) was beheaded the Lady Iane, & with her alſo the Lord Gylforde her huſband, one of the Duke of Northumberlandes ſonnes, two innocentes in compariſon of them that ſat vpon them. For they did but ignorantly accept that which the others had wilfully deuiſed, & by open proclamation conſented to take from others and giue to them.

Touching the condemnation of this lady Iane, here is to be noted, that the Iudge Morgan who gaue the ſentence of condemnation againſt her, ſhortly after hee had condemned her, fell mad, and in his rauing cryed out continually to haue the Lady Iane taken away from him, and ſo ended his lyfe.

And not long after the death of the Lady Iane, vpon the xxi.of the ſame moneth was Henry Duke of Suffolke her father alſo beheaded at the Tower Hyll, the iiij.day after his condemnation: about which tyme alſo were condemned for this conſpiracie many Gentlemē and Yeomen, whereof ſome were executed at London, and ſome in the countrey. In the number of whom was alſo Lorde Thomas Gray, brother to the ſayd Duke, beyng apprehended not long after in North Wales, & executed for y ſame. Syr Nicholas Throgmorton very hardly eſcaped, as ye ſhall heare (the Lorde willing) in an other place.

The xviij.of the ſame moneth, the yeare of our lord 1554. Boner biſhop of London ſent downe a commiſſion, directed to all the Curates and Paſtors of hys Dioces, for the taking of the names of ſuch as would not come the Lent followyng to auricular confeſſion, and to the receiuing at Eaſter: the copie of which monition here followeth.

¶ A monition of Boner biſhop of London, ſent down to all and ſingular Curates of his dioces, for the certyfying of the names of ſuch as would not come in Lent to confeſſion and receiuing at Eaſter.

EDmund by the permiſſion of God, biſhop of London to all Parſons, Uicars, Curates and Miniſters of the Church, within the Citie and dioces of London, ſendeth grace, peace, and mercy, in our Lorde euerlaſtyng. For as much as by the order of the Eccleſiaſticall lawes and conſtitutions of this realme, and the laudable vſage and cuſtome of the whole catholike church, by many hundreth yeares agone, duely and deuoutly obſerued & kept, all faythfull people being of lawfull age and diſcretion, are boūd once in y yeare at leaſt (except reaſonable cauſe excuſe them) to be confeſſed to their own proper Curate, and to receaue the ſacrament of the aultar, with due preparation and deuotion: and for as much alſo as we be credibly informed, that ſundry euill diſpoſed and vndeuout perſons, giuen to ſenſuall pleaſures and carnal appetites, followyng the luſtes of their body, & neglecting vtterly the health of their ſoules, do forbeare to come to confeſſion according to the ſayd vſage, and to receaue the Sacrament of the aultar accordingly, geuing therby pernicious and euyll example to the yonger ſort ſo negligēt and contemne the ſame: we imputing the reformation hereof for our own diſcharge, and deſirous of good order to be kept, and good example to be geuen: do wyt, and commaund you by vertue hereof, that immediately vpon the receipt of this our commaundement, ye and euery ech of you within your cure and charge, doe vſe all

pour diligence and dexteritie to declare the ſame, ſtraitly charging and commaunding all your pariſhioners, being of lawfull age and diſcretion, to come before Eaſter next comming, to confeſſion, according to the ſayd ordinaunce and vſage, and with due preparation and deuotion to receaue the ſayd ſacrament of the aultar, and that ye do note the names of all ſuch as be not confeſſed vnto you & do not receaue of you the ſayd Sacrament, certifying vs of our Chauncellor or Commiſſarie, thereof before the ſixt day of Aprill next enſuing the date hereof: ſo that we knowing therby who did not come to confeſſiō, and receauing the Sacrament accordingly, may procede againſt them, as being perſons culpable, and tranſgreſſours of the ſayd eccleſiaſticall lawe and vſage: Further alſo certifying vs of our ſaid Chauncellor or Commiſſary, before the day aforeſayd, whether ye haue your altars ſet vp, chalice, booke, veſtimentes, and all thinges neceſſary for Maſſe, & the adminiſtration of Sacramēts and ſacramentals, with proceſſion and all other diuine ſeruice prepared and in readines, according to the order of the catholike church, & the vertuous and godly example of the Quenes maieſtye: and if ye ſo haue not, ye then with the church wardens, cauſe the ſame to be prouided for, ſignifying by whoſe fault and negligence the ſame wante or fault hath proceded, and generally of the not comming of your pariſhioners to Church, vndue walking, talking, or vſing of them ſelues there vnreuerently in the tyme of diuine ſeruice, and of al other opē faultes and miſdemeanors, not omitting this to do and certify as before, as you wyll anſwere vpō your peril for the contrary. Geuen at London the xiiij. of February in the yeare of our Lord.1554.

The next moneth folowing, which was the moneth of March, and the iij. day of the ſayd moneth, there was a letter ſent from the Quene to Boner biſhop of London, with certayne articles alſo annexed, to be put in ſpedy execution, containing as here followeth.

¶ Articles ſent frō the Quene to the biſhop of London, by him and his Officers at her commaundement to be put in ſpedy execution, with her letter to the ſayd B.before prefixed

RIght reuerend Father in God, right truſty & welbeloued, we grete you well. And whereas heretofore in the time of the late raigne of our moſt dearest brother king Edward the ſyxt, whoſe ſoule God pardon, diuers notable crimes, exceſſes, and ſchiſmes, with ſundry kindes of hereſies, ſymony, adultery, and other enormities haue bene committed within this our Realme, and other our dominions, the ſame continuyng yet hitherto in like diſorder ſince the beginning of our reigne, without any correction or reformation at all, and the people both of the Laity and alſo of the Clergye, and chiefly of the Clergy haue bene geuen to much diſſolute and vngodly rule, greatly to the diſpleaſure of almighty God, and very much to our regret and euill contentation, and to no litle ſlaunder of other chriſtian realmes: and in maner to the ſubuerſion and clene decaying of this our Realme: and remembring but what to a almightye God to be, to forgiue (as much as in vs and by y char all vertue and godly liuing ſhould be conſeruyd ſo much, & increaſe, and therewith alſo, that all diuers wickedly behauiour ſhould be baniſhed and put away, or at the leaſt wayes, (ſo nygh as might be) ſo bridled and kept vnder, that godlynes with honeſty might thereby ouer hand: vnderſtanding by very credible report & publike fame, to our no ſmall grieuance and diſcomfort, that within your dioces, aſwel in not exempted, as exempted places, the like diſorder and euill behauiour hath bene done and vſed, like alſo to continue and increaſe vnles due prouiſion be had and made to reſtraine the ſame, which earneſtly in very dede we do minde and intend to the vttermoſt all the wayes we can poſſible, truſting of Gods furtherance and helpe in that behalfe: for theſe cauſes, & other moſt iuſt conſiderations vs mouing, we ſend vnto you certayn articles of ſuch ſpeciall matter, as among other thinges be moſt neceſſary to be now put in execution by you and your officeers, according to the end by vs deſired, and the reſormation aforeſayd, wherein ye ſhall be charged with our ſpeciall commaundement, by theſe our letters, to the entent you and your officers may the more earneſtly and boldly procede therinto without feare of any preſumption to be noted on your part, or daunger to be incurred

ſheet. uij.   of

Februarij.

Lady Iane and Lord Galforde Dudley beheaded.

A wonderful example vpon Morgan the Iudge who gaue ſentence againſt the lady Iane.

Feb. xxi.

Henry Duke of Suffolke beheaded.

L. Thomas Gray apprehended and executed.

Feb. 24.

A monition of Boner Biſhop of London to all Miniſters of his Dioces.

Comming to Confeſſion.

Receauing the Sacrament of the Altar.

A letter of Q. Mary to Byſhop Boner.

Cauſes declared.

A Chriſtall Glaſſe for

Chriſtian VVomen.

CONTAINING

A moſte excellent Diſcourſe, of the
Godly life & Chriſtian death of Miſtreſſe Kathe-
rine Stubbes, who departed this life in *Burton* vpon
Trent in *Staffordſhire*, the 14. day of
December.

VVith a moſt heauenly confeſſion of the
Chriſtian Faith which ſhe made a little before her
departure, as alſo a moſte wonderfull combat betwixt Sathan and her ſoule: worthy to be imprinted in Letters of golde, and to be engrauen in the Table
of euery Chriſtian heart.

Set downe word for word as ſhee ſpake it, as neere as could bee gathe-
red: by Phillip Stubbes *Gent.*

REVELA. .14. *verſe* 13.
Bleſſed are the dead that die in the Lord, euen ſo ſaith the
ſpirit, for they reſt from their Labours, and their
workes follow them.

LONDON
Printed for Edward White, and are to bee ſolde at
his ſhop, neere the little North doore of S. Paules
Church at the Signe of the Gun.
1606.

Tu que sancta in ????
beatissima assidis in Caly.
s. Catharina cujus vita purior ????
jam in triumphis ???? ????

A Christall Glasse for Christian VVomen,

wherein they may see moste wonderfull and
rare example of a right vertuous life and Christian death,
as in the discourse following may appeare.

Alling to remembrance (most Christian reader)
the final end of mans creation, which is to glorifie God, and to edifie one another in the way of
true godlines : J thought it my duty, as well in
respect of the one, as in regarde of the other, to
publish this rare and wonderfull example, of the
vertuous life & Christian death of Mistrisse Katherine Stubbes,
who whilst shee liued, was a mirrour of woman-hood, and now
beeing dead, is a perfect patterne of true Christianity. She was
discended of honest & wealthie Parents. Her Father had borne
diuers Offices of worship in his companye, amongst whome he Her Parentage.
liued in good account, credit, and estimation all his daies. Hee
was zealous in the truth, and of a sound Religion. Her Mother
was a Dutchwoman, both discreete and wise , of singular good
grace & modestie, & which did moste of all adorne her, shee was
both religious and also zealous. This couple liuing together, in
the citie of London many yeares, it pleased God to blesse them
with Childzen of whom this Katherine was youngest saue one.
But as shee was youngest saue one by course of nature : so was
shee not inferiour to any of the rest, or rather far excelled them
all (without comparison) by many degrees in the induments
and quallities of the the minde.

At fifteene yeares of age her Father beeing dead, her Mother Her mariage
bestowed her in marriage to one Maister Phillip Stubbes, with
whome she liued soure yeares, and almost a halfe verie honestly,
& godly, with rare commendations of all y knew her : as wel for
her singular wisdome, as also for her modestie, curtesie, gentlenes, affability, and good gouernement. And aboue all, for her fer-

uent zeale, which she bare to the truth, wherin she seemed to surpasse many, insomuch as if she chanced at any time to be in place where either Papist or Atheists were and heard them talke of religion, what countenance or credit soeuer they seemed to be of, shee would not yeelde a iot, nor giue place vnto them at all, but would most mightily iustifie the truth of God against their blasphemous vntruths & conuince them, yea and confound them by ye testimonies of the word of God. Which thing how could it be otherwise for her whole heart was bet to seeke the Lord, her

Her God'y i.e.

whole delight was to bee conuersant in the Scriptures, & to meditate vpon them day and night. Insomuch ye you could sildome or neuer haue come into her house, and haue found her without a Bible or some other good booke in her hands. And when as she was not reading, she wold spend the time in conferring, talking, & reasoning with her husband of the word of God, & of Religion: asking him, what is the sence of this place? and what is the sence of that? How expound you this place? & how expound you that? What obserue you of this place and what obserue you of that? so that she seemed to be as it were rauished with ye same spirit that

Her loue to the word of God.

Dauid was, when he said, The zeale of thine house hath eaten me vp

She followed the commaundement of our saviour Christ, who biddeth vs to search the Scriptures, for in them yee hope to haue eternall life. She obeyed the commaundement of the Apostle, who biddeth women to be silent, & to learne of their husbands at home. She would neuer suffer any disorder or abuse in her house to be either vnreproued or vnreformed. And so gentle was she, & curteous of nature, that she was neuer heard to giue any the lie in all her life nor so much as to (thou) any in anger: She

Her gentlenesse.

was neuer known to fal out with any of her neighbours nor with the least Childe ye liued much lesse to scould or brawle, as many wil now a daies, for euerie trifle or rather for no cause at all: and so solitarily was she giuen, that she wold very sildome or neuer, and then not neither, except her husband were in company, goe abroad with any eyther to banquet or feast, to Gossip or make merrie, as they tearme it, insomuch that she was noted by some though most vntruely, to doe it in contempt & disdain of others.

When her husband was abroad at London, or els where, there was not the dearest friend she had in the world, ye could get her
abroad

abroad to dinner or ſupper, to playes, or interludes, nor to any
other paſtimes or diſportes whatſoeuer: neither was ſhe giuen
to pamper her bodie with delicate meates, wine or ſtrong drink,
but rather refrained them altogether, ſaying: that we ſhold eate
to liue, & not liue to eate. And as ſhe excelled in the gift of ſobrie-
ty, ſo ſhe ſurpaſſed in ẙ vertue of humilitie. For it is wel known
to diuers yet liuing, that ſhee vtterly abhorred all kinde of pride
as wel in apparel as otherwiſe. She could neuer abide to heare
any filthy or vnſeemly talke of ſcurilitie, bawderie, or vncleanes, neither ſwearing nor blaſpheming, curſing, nor banning, Her integrity of life.
but wold reprooue them ſharply, ſhewing thē the vengeance of
God due for ſuch deſerts. And which is more, there was neuer
one filthy, vncleane, vndecent, or vnſeemely word heard to come
forth of her mouth, nor neuer once to curſe or banne, to ſweare,
or blaſpheme God any māner of way, but alwaies her ſpēches
were ſuch, as both might glorifie God, and miniſter grace to the
hearers as the Apoſtle ſpeaketh. And for her conuerſation, there
was neuer any man or woman that euer opened their mouthes
againſt her, or that euer did, or could once accuſe her of the leaſt
ſhaddowe of diſhoneſtie, ſo continently ſhe liued, and ſo circum-
ſpectly ſhe walked, eſchewing euen the verie outward appea-
rance or ſhew of euill.

Againe, for true loue and loyaltie to her huſband, and his
friendes, ſhe was (let me ſpeake it without offence) I think the
rareſt Paragon in the world: for ſhee was ſo farre from diſ-
wading her huſband to bee beneficiall to his friendes, that ſhee
would rather perſwade him to bee more beneficiall to them. If
ſhe ſaw her huſband to be merry, then ſhe was merry: if he were
heauie or paſſionate, ſhe would indeuour to make him glad: if he
were angry ſhe wold quickely pleaſe him, ſo wiſely ſhe demea-
ned herſelfe towards him. She wold neuer contrary him in any Her demea-nor toward her husband.
thing, but by wiſe counſell and ſage aduiſe, and with all humili-
tie, & ſubmiſſion ſeek to perſwade him. And alſo little giuen was
ſhee to this world, that ſome of her neighbours maruailing why
ſhe was no more carefull of it, would aſke her ſometimes, ſay-
ing: Miſtreſſe Stubbes, why are you no more carefull for the Her little care of the world.
thinges of this life, but ſitte alwaies poaring vpon a booke, and
reading? to whome ſhee would anſwere, If I ſhould be a friend

vnto

unto this world, I should bee an enemie vnto God: for God and the world, are two contraries. Iohn biddeth mee, loue not the world nor any thing in the world, affirming that if I loue the world the loue of the father is not in me. Againe christ biddeth me, first seeke the kingdome of Heauen, and the righteousnes thereof and then all those worldly thinges shall be giuen to me, Godlines is great ritches if a man be content with ý he hath. I haue chosen with good Mary, the better part which shall neuer bee taken from mee. Gods treasure shee would say is neuer drawne drie. I haue enough in this life, God make me thankfull, and I knowe I haue but a short time to liue heere, and it standeth mee vppon to haue regard to my saluation in the life to come Thus this Godly young Gentlewoman held on her course three or foure yeares after shee was married: at which time it pleased God that she conceiued with a man Childe, after which conception she would say to her her husband, and many other her good neighbours and friendes yet liuing, not once nor twice, but many times, that shee should neuer beare moe Children: that, that Childe should be her death, and that shee should liue but to bring that Childe into the world. Which thing no doubt was reuealed vnto her by the spirit of God, for according to her prophecie so it came to passe.

Her prophecie of her death.

The time of her account beeing come, she was deliuered of a goodly man Childe, with as much speede, and as safely in al womens iudgements as any could be. And after her deliuerie, shee grew so strong, that shee was able within foure or fiue daies to sitte vp in her bed, and to walke vp and downe her chamber, and within a fortnight to goe abroad in the house: being throughly well, and past all danger, as euerie one thought. But presently vppon this so suddaine recouerie, it pleased God to visite her againe with an extreame hot & burning quotidiã Ague, in which shee languished for the space of sire weekes or there abouts. During all which time, shee was neuer seene or perceiued to sleepe one houre together, neither night nor day, and yet the Lord kept her (which was miraculous) in her perfect vnderstanding, sence, and memorie to the last breath, praysed bee his holy name therfore. In all her sickenes, which was both long and greeuous, she neuer shewed any signe of discontentment or impatience, nei-

Her deliuerie of Childe.

Her sickenes.

ther

ther was there euer heard one word come foorth of her mouth
sounding eyther of desperation or infidelitie: of mistrust or dist-
rust, or of any doubting or wauering, but alwaies remained
faithfull and resolute in her God. And so desirous was she to bee
with the Lord, that these golden sentences were neuer out of her
mouth, I desire to be dissolued and to be with Christ. And O miserable wretch þ I am, who shal deliuer me from this body subiect to sin? Come quickly Lord Iesus, come quickly. Like as the
Hart desireth þ water springs, so doth my soule thirst after thé.
O God I had rather bee a doore keeper in the house of my God
thé to dwel in þ tents of the wicked: with many other heauenly
Her desire to
bee with god
sentences, which least I shold séeme tedious, I willingly omit.
Her absolute
prayer for
death.
She would alwaies pray in her sicknes absolutely, þ God wold
take her out of this miserable world. And when her husband & o-
thers, wold desire her to pray for health if it were þ wil of God,
She would answere, I beseech you pray not that I should liue,
for I thinke it long to be with my God. Christ is to me life, and
death is to me aduantage, yea the day of death is the birth day of
euerlasting life. And I cãnot enter into life but by death, therfore
is death the doore or entrance into euerlasting life to me. I know
& am certainely perswaded by the spirit of God, þ the sentence is
giuen already by þ great iudge, in the court or parlament of heauen, þ I shal now depart out of this life, & therefore pray not for
me þ I might liue here, but pray to God to giue me strength and
patience to perseuer to þ end, & to close mine eyes in a iustifying
faith in the blood of my Christ. Sometimes she would speak verie softly to her selfe, and sometimes very audible these wordes,
doubling thé a hundred times together. Oh my good God, why
not now? why not now? Oh my good God, I am readye for
thee, I am prepared: Oh receiue me now for thy Christes sake.
Oh send thy messenger death to fetch me, send thy Sergeant to
arrest mee, thy Purseuant to attach me, thy Harrald to summõ
me. O send thy Iaylor to deliuer my soule out of prison, for my
bodie is nothing else but a stinking prison to my soule. Oh send
thine holy Angels to conduct my soule into þ euerlasting kingdome of heauen. Other sometimes shee would lie as it were in
a slumber, her eyes closed, and her lips vttering these words very softly to her selfe: O my sweete Iesus, O my loue Iesus,
why

Her Godly meditation.

why not now? sweet Jesus, why not now? O sweet Jesus pray for me, pray for mee sweet Jesus. repeating them many times together These and infinit the like were her dayly speeches and continual meditations, and neuer worser word was there heard to come forth of her mouth during al the time of her sicknes. She was accustomed many times as she lay, verie suddainely to fall into a sweete smiling, and sometimes into a moste heartie laughter, her face appearing right faire, red, amiable, and louely,

Her glorious visions:

and her countenance seemed as though shee greatly reioyced at some glorious sight. And when her husband wold aske her why she smiled and laughed so? She would say, oh if you saw such glorious and heauenly sights as I see, you would reioyce and laugh with me: for I see a vision of the ioyes of heauen, and of the glorie y I shall goe vnto: and I see infinite millions of Angels, attendant vpon me, and watching ouer me, readie to carry my soule into the kingdome of heauen. In regarde whereof shee was willing to forsake her selfe, her husband, her childe, and all the world besides. And so calling for her childe, which the Nurse brought vnto her: shee tooke it in her armes, and kissing it, said: God blesse thee (my sweete Babe) & make thee an heire of the kingdome of heauen, and kissing it againe deliuered it to the Nurse, with these wordes to her husband standing by. Beloued

Her request to her Husband for the bringing vp of her childe.

husband, I bequeath this my childe vnto you, hee is no longer mine, he is the Lordes and yours. I forsake him, you, and all the world, yea and mine owne selfe, & esteeme all thinges but dung, that I may win Jesus Christ. And I pray you sweete husband, bring vp this childe in good letters, in learning and discipline, and aboue all thinges, see that he be brought vp, and instructed in the exercise of true Religion.

The childe being taken away, she espyed a little Puppye or

Her hatred to the world.

Bitch (which in her life time she loued well) lying vpon her bed, she had no sooner espied her, but she beate her away, and calling her husband to her, said: good Husband, you and I haue offended God grieuously in receiuing this bitch many a time into our bed, we wold haue been loath to haue receiued a Christian soule, purchased with the precious blod of Jesus Christ into our bed, & to haue nourished him in our bosomes, & to haue fed him at our Table, as we haue done this filthy cur many times, the

Lord

Lord giue vs grace to repent it, and al other vanities. And afterward could ſhe neuer abide to looke vppon the Witch any more. Hauing thus Godly diſpoſed of all things, ſhe fel into a traunce or ſwound for the ſpace almoſte of a quarter of an houre, ſo as euerie one thought ſhe had been dead: But afterward ſhee comming to herſelfe ſpake to them that were preſent (as there were many both worſhipfull and others) ſaying: right worſhipful & my good neigbbours and friendes, I thanke you al for the great paines you haue taken with me, in this bed of my ſicknes: and wheras I am not able to requite you, I beſeech the Lord to reward you in the kingdome of heauen. And for that my houre glaſſe is runne out, and that my time of departure hence is at hand: I am perſwaded for three cauſes to make a confeſſion of my faith before you all. The firſt cauſe that mooueth me hereto is, for that thoſe (if there be any ſuch here) y are not yet throughly reſolued in the truth of God, may heare and learne what the ſpirit of God hath taught mee out of his bleſſed and all ſauing word. The ſecond cauſe that mooueth mee, is, for that none of you ſhould iudge that I dyed not a perfect Chriſtian and a liuely member of the miſticall body of Ieſus Chriſt, and ſo by your raſh iudgement might incurre the diſpleaſure of God. The third and laſt cauſe is, for that as you haue beene witneſſes of part of my life, ſo you might be witneſſes of part of my faith and belæfe alſo. And in this my confeſſion, I would not haue you to thinke that it is I that ſpeake vnto you, but the ſpirit of God which dwelleth in me, and in all the elect of God, vnleſſe they be reprobates: For Paul ſaith Rom. 8. If any one haue not the Spirit of Chriſt dwelling in him, he is none of his. This bleſſed ſpirit hath knocked at the doore of my heart, and my God hath giuen me grace to open the doore vnto him, and hee dwelleth in mee plentifully. And therefore I pray you giue me patience a little, and imprint my words in your harts, for they are not the words of fleſh and blood, but the ſpirit of God by whome we are ſealed to the day of our redemption.

B   A moſte

A moste heauenly confession of the Christian faith, made by the blessed Seruant of God, Mistris *Katherine Stubbes*, a little before she dyed.

Lthough the Maiestie of God be both infinite and vnspeakeable, and therefore according to his excellent dignitie can neither be conceaued in heart nor expressed in wordes, yet to the end you may knowe what God is, in whome I beleeue, as farre as he hath reuealed himself vnto vs in his holy word, I will define him vnto you as the spirit of God shall illuminate my heart. I beleeue therefore with my heart & freely confesse with my mouth heere before you all, that this God in whome I beleeue, is a moste glorious spirit, or spirituall substance, a diuine essence, or essential being, without beginning or ending, of infinite glorie, power, might, & maiesty: inuisible inaccessible, incomprehensible, & altogether vnspeakeable. I beleeue and confesse that this glorious God-head, this blessed substance, essence or beeing, this diuine power which wee call God, is diuided into a Trinitie of persons, the Father, the Sonne and the holy Spirit, distinct onely in names and offices, but all one, and the same in nature, in essence, substance, deitie, maiestie, power, might, and eternitie. I beleeue and confesse, that God the Father the first person in this blessed Trinitie, is from euerlasting, before and beyond all times, not made, nor created, nor begotten of any, but the onely Maker, Creator, and begetter of all thinges whatsoeuer. I beleeue and confesse that Iesus Christ the Sonne of God is the second person in this glorious Trinitie, not created nor made of any, but begotten of his Father before all eternitie, time, or worlds. I beleeue the holy Spirit to bee the third person in this sacred Trinitie, not made of any nor begotten, but proceeding both from the Father and the Sonne, as the verie wisdome, and inspiration of them both. I doe beleeue and confesse that this moste glorious Trinitie is consubstantiall and coessentiall together, none before or after other, none greater or lesser then other, of equall power, of equall Maiestie, of equall glorie, and eternitie, (as before.)

fore.) I beleeue and confesse, that this God, this blessed Trinitie, not onely created all things both visible & inuisible, spirituall
and corporall, where or whatsoeuer, but also that he vpholdeth,
continueth and maintaineth them by his almightie power and
vnsearchable wisdome, through the secret working of his spirit.
I beleeue and confesse that this great God ordereth and dispo-
seth all thinges, according to his good pleasure and wil, and that
he also foreseeth and foreknoweth all thinges, according to his
prouidence, and prescience, so that nothing commeth to passe by
fortune, chance, or casualtie to him, though it seemeth fortunall *No fortune*
or casual to vs, who see neither the beginnings, the middles, the *or chance.*
entes, the causes, nor effects of things before they come to passe.
I beleeue and confesse that the Lord our God, hauing created
the vniuersall engine and frame of this world, with all thinges
contained therein, for the benefit and vse of man, the last of all o-
ther creatures, euen the sirt day created man after his owne si-
militude and likenesse, holy, pure, good, innocent, and in euerie
part perfect and absolute, giuing him also wisdome, discretion, *Mans perfec-*
vnderstanding and knowledge aboue all other creatures, (the *tion.*
holy Angels onely excepted) and which was more, he gaue vnto
him a certaine power, strength, facultie (which we cal free-wil)
by force whereof he might haue continued and remained for e-
uer in his integritie, and holynes if he had would. But hee had
no sooner receiued this inestimable blessing of free-wull, of innocencie, and integritie, but by harkning to the poysoned suggestions of the wicked Serpent, and by obeying his perswasi-
ons, he lost his free-wull, his integritie, and perfection, and vs all
his posteritie to the end of the world, and so of a Saint in heauen, hee (and wee in him) became fire-brandes of hell, vassailes *Mans fall*
of Sathen, Miscreants, Reprobates, Abiectes, and Castawaies
before the face of God for euer. Then when there was no o-
ther way or meanes for men to bee saued in the Iustice of God:
I doe constantlye beleeue and confesse that God the Father in
the multitude of his mercies, when the fulnesse of time was
come, sent his owne Sonne Christ Iesus, forth of his owne bo- *Christ his in-*
some into this miserable world, to take our nature vpon him, *carnation.*
and that in the wombe of a Virgin without spot or blemish of
sinne, and without the helpe of man, by the wonderful opera-

B 2   tion

tion and ouershadowing of the holy Ghost.

And as I constantly beleeue that Jesus Christ is come in the flesh (according to the Scriptures) so I vnfainedly beleeue ý he hath offered vp his blessed body vpon the Alter of ý Crosse, as a Sacrifice propitiatorie, satisfactorie, & expiatory, for the sins of the whole world, and for mee the chiefest of all sinners: By vertue, power, and efficacie, of which Sacrifice and oblation onely, I trust and beleeue to bee saued, and by the merrits of the blood of this immaculate Lambe (Christ Jesus) to bee sette free, and pardoned of all my sinnes whatsoeuer. And whereas the professed enemies of GOD, the Papistes doe bragge of their good workes, of their merrites, righteousnesse and desertes: I heere before you all, in the presence of God, and his holy Angels, doe vtterly renounce, abandon and forsake all my owne merrits, righteousnes & deserts, as filthy dung: acknowledging my merrits to bee the merrits of God in Christ, who is made vnto me righteousnes, holines, sanctification and redemption. For I am assured that if the Lord should weigh my righteousnes in the ballance of his iustice, rewarding me according to the same, I shold receiue nothing but iust damnation for my deserts. I doe further beleeue and confesse that Jesus Christ hauing suffered death vpon the Crosse for me and all mankinde, rose againe to life the third day after, by the spirituall power of his God-head conquering thereby sinne, death, hell Sathan and al his hellish band. I doe also beleeue that the same Jesus Christ after his moste victorious resurrection ascended into heauen, in the sight of the Apostles and holy Saints, a cloud receiuing him out of their sight, there not onely to prepare a place for vs, but also to make continuall prayer and intercession for vs to God the Father, at whose right hand he now sitteth, in equall glory and blisse for euermore.

I doe constantly beleeue that the heauens must holde his corporal presence, till the day of iudgement: that his blessed body is circumscriptible, and contained in one local place, and cannot be present in euerie place, at one and the same time: his Deity and his God-head, notwithstanding being in euerie place at once, & fulfilling all places, and yet contained in no one place. For it is against the nature of a true bodie to bee present in many places

at

[marginal note: ...rist his ...ice.]

[marginal note: ...rist his resurrection.]

[marginal note: ...rist his ascension.]

[marginal note: The heauens must holde Christs essentiall bodie til the day of iudgement.]

at once : and therefore the Papistes in effect denye the bodie of Christ to be a true essentiall and naturall bodie, by teaching it to be present in their so many and sundrie places at once.

I doe also beleeue and confesse, that this Iesus Christ shall come at the latter day of iudgement (when the number of Gods elect shall be fulfilled) in the same liknes that he was seene goe vp into heauen & with the same naturall bodie, to iudge both the quicke and the dead, and reward euerie man according to his workes. At which day I doe constantly beleeue, that all flesh, I meane of mankind only, shal rise againe by ye omnipotent power of God, whereby hee is able to subdue all things to himselfe, not one haire of their heades lacking. Then death shall yeeld vp his dead, the graue his dead, ye sea his dead, and hel his dead. And then shal the soules of the Godly, of the elect & chosen of God enter into their own bodies again, & be reunited together, their bodies now being renued, altered & changed : for being before corruptible bodies, they shall now be made incorruptible: being before mortal bodies, now they shall be made immortall: being before filthie and vncleane, they shall now be made cleane & pure like to the glorious body of Christ Iesus, shining as the Sunne for euer in the kingdome of heauen, where they shall dwell for euer, in such ioy as no heart can thinke, nor tongue expresse, nor pen is able to write. Vpon the other side, the soules of the wicked and reprobate shall be reunited to their proper bodies, and both together shall bee cast into hell fire, where is nothing but weeping, wayling, and gnashing of teeth for euermore.

Christ comming to iudgement & of our resurrection.

Furthermore I beleeue and confesse, that the soules of al the elect Children of God, immediately after their departure out of their bodies, do goe into ye kingdom of heauen, into the hands of God, being guided & conducted thither by the ministry of the angels of God, and not in purgatorie, Limbo patrum, or any other place whatsoeuer. For whither the soule of Christ was receiued when he cryed Father, into thy hands I commend my Spirit, thither are the soules of all the Children of God, that die in the true faith of Iesus Christ, receiued immediately after their departure hence. In the Gospell after Saint Luke, we reade that the soule of poore Lazarus, or blessed Lazarus, streight after his death, was carryed into heauen by the angels of God, & not into

Whether the soules of the faithfull doe go after their departure out of their bodies.

Popish

Popish purgatorie, which was not hatched almosse of two hundred yeares after. The soule of the penitent and faithfull theefe was carryed straight way into paradice, for so Christ told him: This day shalt thou be with me in paradice: ý is, the kingdome of heauen, and not in purgatorie. Salomon saith, chapter 3. The soules of the righteous are in the hands of God, and there shall no torments come nigh them. Christ saith, hee went into heauen to prepare a place for vs, and then not into purgatorie except they will haue their purgatory to be in heauen.

He saith further that where he is there shall his Seruants be also. But I hope they will not say that Christ is in Purgatory, but in heauen, and thither shall all the soules of the faithfull ascend immediatly, and therfore is the opinion of Popish purgatorie both blasphemous and sacrilegious. But the true purgatorie indeede is this, the blood of Iesus Christ, which clenseth vs from all sinne: no other purgatorie doe I know of by the word of God, nor acknowledge. I beleeue also and confesse, that man is iustifyed, that is, pronounced iust before God, freed from sin and all punishments due for sinne, by a true and liuely faith in the blood of Christ onely, and not by his workes, merrits, righteousnesse, or desertes: neither yet by any inherent righteousnes in himselfe, as the blasphemous Papistes teach, nor by anye other meanes whatsoeuer. And therefore the Apostle to the Rom 4. was bold to say that if Abraham were iustifyed by workes, then had he wherein to reioyce, but not with God, for hee saith afterward in the 5. Chapter, being iustifyed by faith we haue peace toward God through Iesus Christ. And therefore doe I constantly beleeue, that wee are iustifyed by faith onely, and not by the workes of the law. For if good workes could saue vs, thē had christ dyed in vaine. And if they could saue vs, why should they not be called by the name of our sauiours? But when I say that faith onely iustifyeth I meane not a barren faith or a dead faith, without good workes, such as the Deuils haue: But I speake of such a faith as bringeth foorth good workes in great plentie: and can no more bee without good workes, then the Sunne without light, the fire without heate, or the water without his naturall moysture. If you would know why we should doe good workes if we cannot bee saued

by

Purgatory of the Papists blasphemous.

Man iustified by faith only.

by them , I will tell you: wee must doe good works for foure causes chiefely. First to shew our obedience to him that commaunds vs. Secondly, to glorifie him that created vs, and ordained good workes: also that we shold walke in them. Thirdly for the mutual loue and charitie which we beare towards our Bretheren: Fourthly to make our saluation sure and certaine vnto vs, as the Apostle speaketh. For these & other causes must we doe good workes, and yet we must not trust to bee saued by them, for there is no other name giuen vnder heauen, whereby a man can bee saued, but onely the name of Iesus Christ. I doe also constantly beleue and confesse, that al the canonicall scriptures are the infallible word of God, & that the holy spirit of god was and is the onely author of them, and that holy men of God spake and writ them as they were taught and inspired by the spirit of God, as blessed Peter beareth recorde. I also beleeue that the holy Scriptures doe containe all thinges necessarie to saluation, without all Popish trash of vnwritten verities, or rather vnwritten verie lies. I doe further also beleeue & confesse that God the Father hath from euerlasting & before al worldes, in his secret councell, and in his euerlasting purpose and decrée, elected, chosen, and predestinate in Christ Iesus, certaine of the lost Sonnes of Adam, to bee members of his bodie, and coheires with him of his heauenly Kingdome. And other some hath bee predestinated to euerlasting destruction, leauing them in their naturall sinne, and corruption still. Now if you aske me what predestination and reprobation is: I answere, it is the euerlasting purpose and decree of God whereby he dooth choose some to saluation , and some to damnation. If you demaund why hee chooseth some to saluation, and not all, finding them all in like state and condition: I answere. In choosing of some to saluation, he sheweth his vnspeakeable mercie, grace, fauour and loue, and in choosing othersome to damnation, he sheweth his power, his iustice, and his iudgement to al the world. For as by the one the mercy of god appeareth, so by the other we may sée what we haue all deserued. And if you aske me yet, why hee chooseth some and reiecteth othersome, I tell you, he may doe it at his blessed will & pleasure. For if I haue two debters that owe me a thousand pound a peece, it is in me to release the one of the whole debt,

and

Why we should doe good works

The canonical scripture the inuisible word of God

Her faith in the predestinatió of God, & what it is.

and to exact the whole of ȳ other: for to the one I shew but mercie, and to the other but iustice. Now those ȳ the Lord hath predestinate in Christ Iesus to euerlasting saluation, them doth he cal in his good time to the knowledge of his truth, to repentãce, to integritie, to life and to al perfection: and those whom he doth cal, them doth he iustifie: and whome he dooth iustifie, them wil he glorifie. And that doctrine of predestination and reprobation standeth thus: the Apostle Eph. 1.11. sheweth euidently, saying: We are chosen in christ, when we were predestinate according to ȳ purpose of him that worketh al things after the councell of his will: and in the 4. and 5. vers. of the same Chapter, he saith: Wee are chosen in him, meaning Christ, before the foundation of the world, that wee should bee holy and blamelesse before him in loue. Reade Romaines 9. and many other places of holy scriptures, & you shal finde this doctrine to be very cleare. I doe further beleeue & confesse that God hath his seuerall churches, and namely his church tryumphant in ȳ the kingdome of heauen, & his church millitant dispersed vpon the face of ȳ earth. I doe also beleeue, that this millitant church is two fold, visible and inuisible. The visible Church is knowne and discerned by these markes: the word of God preached, ȳ sacraments sincerely ministred, & Ecclesiasticall discipline and other censures of the church duely executed. The other Church, I call the inuisible church, not for that men are inuisible, but for that it alwaies appeareth not to the eye of the world, but is knowne to God onely who alone knoweth who are his. I beleeue ȳ this church, this spouse of Christ cannot erre finally in matters of saluation, and damnation, so long as she holdeth her head Christ Iesus aright. And I constantly beleeue, ȳ Iesus Christ is the onely head, ruler and gouernour of this Church, and not Antichrist the Pope, nor any of his chanelings: as Paul testifieth. Ephe. 4.15. saying let vs grow vp in al things, in him who is the head Iesus christ: Againe, in an other place, hee saith: as Christ is the head of the Church, so is the husband head ouer his wife. I beleeue and confesse, that Iesus Christ hath left, not only the holy Scriptures to instruct and teach his church, but also sacraments in number two: to wit, Baptisme and the Lords Supper, as seales of his grace towards it, to confirme it in his truth, and as conduits of

his

Marginal notes:
- Our vocation or calling.
- The Church two folde & how.
- How & when the Church cannot erre.
- Christ is the sole head of the Church.

his mercie, to conuey his grace and goodnes to it also.

These Sacraments I say, are seales & signes of holy thinges, and therfore cannot be the things themselues. For it is against the nature of a sacrament, to be the thing signified therby. Baptisme consisteth of two natures, the visible element, and the inuisible grace. The visible element is water: the inuisible grace are the giftes and graces of the holy Ghost, confirmed in Baptisme. The water signifyeth vnto vs that our whole nature is corrupted, and had neede to be purged and clensed. It signifieth also vnto vs, our regeneration, sanctification, and new birth. And it represēteth also vnto vs the blood of Iesus Christ, which clenseth vs from all sinnes. And I faithfully beleeue that it is no more lawfull for a woman to minister this Sacrament, then it is lawfull for her to preach, or to minister the Sacrament of the Lords supper.

And as concerning the Sacrament of the Lords supper, I beleeue & confes, that it consisteth of two natures also: an earthly and an heauenly Nature or qualitie. The visible Element or earthly nature is Bread & wine: the heauenly nature or qualitie, the bodie and blood of Christ signified therby. The wine doth represent vnto vs the blood of Christ, which was shed for vs: and the bread dooth signifie vnto vs also, the bodie of Christ, which was giuen for vs. And as many as receiue this sacrament worthily, in remembrance of the death and passion of Iesus Christ, doe eate and drink Iesus Christ (spiritually) to their eternal saluation. And I doe verily beleeue, that in this sacrament, neither the bread nor the wine, neither before nor after the wordes of consecration (as they tearme them) are changed, altered, or transubstantiat into the reall, essentiall, or materiall body of Christ. but remaine the same still in nature and substance that they were before. And therefore Paul feared not to call it bread still, many times, in his epistle to the Corinthians. And our Sauiour in the 6. of S. Iohn, saith: that they should see him ascend into heauen, with the same bodie that he sat in with them at Supper, whole and vneaten: adding further, that the wordes that hee spake were spirit and truth: and that it is the spirit that giueth life, the flesh profiteth little. And he biddeth vs to celebrate this supper in remembraece of him: and to preach his death therein till

C

he

Side notes:

Two Sacramentes, and what they are, wherof they dou consist, and what they represent vntovs.

Neither the bread nor wine changed in the Lords Supper.

he come againe. If Christ were in the Sacrament, flesh and blood, and bone, then the wicked might eate him, and so should there neuer any wicked bee condemned. For Christ saith, he that eateth his flesh, and drinketh his blood shall neuer die, yea Rats, Cats, and Mice might eate his body, which were blasphemous and sacrilegions once to imagine, though the Papists are not ashamed to teach it openly. And albeit y these Sacraments doe represent vnto vs moste excellent thinges, yet doe they not confer grace of themselues, neither is the grace of God so tyed to the materiall elements, that hee cannot saue without them. And therefore are the Papistes more then cruell, that teach, all Children to be damned that die before baptisme. For wee reade of certaine in the Actes of the Apostles, that were baptized, and yet they had not so much as heard whether there were any holy Ghost or not. Simon Magus was baptized, yet he receiued not the holy Ghost thoe. And againe, Cornelius had receiued the holy Ghost before his baptisme. Iohn the Baptist receiued the holy Ghost in his Mothers wombe, and the like. But yet notwithstanding although the grace of God bee not tyed to the sacraments, yet hee that may receiue them, and will not , or else setteth light by them, shall neuer receiue the giftes and graces signified by them.

I doe also most constantly beleeue. that as Iesus Christ is the vndoubted sauiour of the world, so is he our onely Mediator, aduocate, and intercessour of God the Father, & none but he alone who is ascended into the heauens , sitteth on the right hand of God, & maketh continuall prayers to God for vs. As Iohn saith: If any man sinnes, we haue an aduocate with the father Iesus Christ the righteous, and he is the propitiation for our sinnes. And to the same effect Paul speaketh. 1. Tim. 2. 5. There is one God, and one Mediator betweene God and man, which is the man Christ Iesus. And as I beleeue that Iesus Christ is our onely mediator and aduocate, so I constantly beleeue that he is onelye to bee called vpon, innocated and prayed vnto, and neither Saint nor angell, Patriarcke. nor Father. Martir, nor confessour, Peter nor Paul, Apostle. nor Euangelist, Iames nor Iohn, no not Mary her selfe, nor any other creature how excellēt soeuer they seemed to be in the eyes of the world. For wee are

assured

Sacraments doe not conferre grace.

Christ is our onely Mediator.

Christ onely to be called vpon, & not Saints.

assured by the word of God, that the Saintes can neither heare our prayers, nor graunt our requests, and therfore Christ saith: Call vpon me in the day of thy trouble, and I will deliuer thee, & thou shalt praise me. And againe, the Apostle saith, How shal they call vpon him, in whome they haue not beleeued: Then as it is not lawfull to beleeue in any other saue in God alone, so it is not lawfull to pray to any other, saue to God alone, in the name and mediation of Christ Iesus onely.

I doe also moste constantly beleeue, that my soule, so soone as euer it departeth out of my body, shal be carried by the ministry of the holy angels of God in to the kingdome of heauen: where I shal see & certainly know, Adam Euah, Noah, Abraham, Isack, Iacob, Moses, Samuel, Dauid, & all other Prophets, Patriarks, and Fathers, together with Mary the Mother of Christ. Peter, Paul, Iames and Iohn, and all other Martirs, Confessours, and holy Saintes of God, which haue dyed since the beginning of the world, or which shall die to the end of the same. Oh what a comfortable thing is this, that we shal know one another, in the life to come, talke with one another, loue one another, & praise God one with another, and altogether world without end! And because some of you peraduenture will hardly beleeue this doctrine to be so, I pray you giue me leaue to prooue it by the word of God, and then I will make an end.

Her beleefe whether her soule should see after her departure.

When God cast Adam into a dead sleepe, and made woman of a rib of his side, hee brought her vnto him, and hee knewe her straite way, & he called her by her name. Could Adam in y state of innocency know his wife, he being in a dead sleepe whilst she was in making: and shall not we, being restored to a far more excellent dignitie and perfection, then euer Adam was in, not knowe one another? shal our knowledge be lesse in heauen then it is in earth? doe we not know one another in this life, where we know but in part, we see but in part, yea as it were in a glasse: and shall wee not know one another in the life to come, where all ignorance shall be done away?

We shall knowe one another in the life to come.

We shall bee like (saith Christ) the glorious Angels which know one another, & shall not we then know one another in the life to come? Shall we be like them in other things, & faile onely in this? We shal, saith the apostle, see and know Christ, euen as

he

he is, who is the wisdome, image, and brightnes of his Fathers substance, and shal not we know one another? We are al members of one bodie, & shall not wee know one another? Christ Iesus is our head, and wee his members, and shall not the members know their head, and so consequently one another? They that are all fellow-seruants in one house but for a short time in this world doe know one another, and shall not wee knowe one another after this life being fellowe Cittizens in one & the same Cittie, subiects in one & the same kingdome, & seruing one Lord and Maister with one spirit and minde for euer world without end? Shal brute beastes knowe one another in this life, and shal not wee knowe one another, seeing God face to face, in knowledge of whome consisteth all knowledge? The Apostles knew Christ after he was risen againe and shal not we know one another after the generall resurrection of the flesh?

In the 16. of Luke we reade, how that the rich man lying in hell, knew Abraham and Lazarus in heauen a far off. Then I reason thus : if the wicked that be in hell, in torments, doe know those that be in heauen so farre aboue, how much more shall the Godly know one another, being altogether in one place, and felow Cittizens in the kingdom of heauen? We reade also in p̄ 17 of Mar. how our Sauiour Christ meaning to shew vnto his disciples. Peter, Iames, & Iohn, as it were a shadow, or glimmering of the ioyes of heauen, and therefore he is said to bee transfigured before them, and his face did shine as the Sunne, his apparell was like the light, there appeared vnto them Moses & Elias, saith p̄ text. Then it followeth that if the Disciples being in their natural corruption, & but in a shadow or glimmering of the ioyes of heauen did know Moses & Elias, the one whereof dyed almost two thousand yeres before, & the other not much lesse: how much more shall wee know one another in the life to come, all corruption being taken away, and wee in the full fruition & possession of all the ioyes and glorie of heauen? This is my faith, this is my hope, and this is my trust, this hath the spirit of God taught me, and this haue we learned out of the booke of God. And good Lord, that hast begun this good worke in me, finish it, I beseech thee, and strengthen me, that I may perseuer therein to the end, and in the end, through Iesus Christ my onely Lord & sauiour.

She had no sooner made an end of this moste heauenly con-
feſſion of her faith, but ſathan was readie to bid her the combat, Sathan tempteth her.
whome ſhe mightily repulſed ⁊ vanquiſhed by the power of our
Lord Ieſus, on whome ſhee conſtantly belieued : and whereas
before ſhe looked with a ſweet, louely, and amiable countenance,
red as the roſe, and moſte beautifull to beholde: now vppon the
ſuddaine ſhe bent her browes, ſhe frowned, ⁊ looking as it were
with an angrie ſterne, and auſtere countenance, as though ſhæ
ſaw ſome filthie vggleſome ⁊ diſpleaſant thing, ſhee burſt forth
into theſe ſpeeches following, pronouncing her wordes ſcorne-
fully, and diſdainefully, in contempt of him to whome ſhe ſpake.

A moſte wonderfull conflict betwixt Sathan and her ſoule, and
of her valiant conqueſt in the ſame, by the power
of Chriſt.

HOw now ſathan, what makeſt ÿ heere ⁊ Art thou come to
tempt th Lords ſeruant? I tel thee (thou hell hound) thou Her woo-derfull ten-tation and valiant con-queſt in the ſame.
haſt no part nor portion in mee, nor by the grace of God neuer
ſhalt haue, I was, now am, and ſhal be the Lords for euer, yea
(ſathan) I was choſen ⁊ elected in Chriſt to euerlaſting ſaluati-
on, before the foundations of the world were laide, ⁊ therefore,
thou maiſt get thæ packing, thou damned dog, ⁊ goe ſhake thine
eares, for in me thou haſt naught. But what doeſt ÿ lay to my
charge, thou foule fiend? Oh, that I am a ſinner, ⁊ therfore ſhall
be damned. I confeſſe indeed that I am a ſinner, and a greuous
ſinner, both by original ſin, and actuall ſin, ⁊ that I may thanke
thee for. And therefore ſathan I bequeath my ſinne to thæ from
whence it firſt came, ⁊ I appeale to the mercy of God in Chriſt
Ieſus. Chriſt came to ſaue ſinners as he ſaith himſelfe, ⁊ not the
righteous : behold the Lambe of God, ſaith Iohn ÿ taketh away
the ſins of the world: And in another place he cryeth out, ÿ blood
of Ieſus Chriſt doth clenſe vs from all ſin. And therefore ſathan
I conſtantly beleeue that my ſins are waſhed away in the precious blood of Ieſus Chriſt, ⁊ ſhall neuer be imputed to me any
more. But what ſaiſt thou more, ſathan, doeſt thou aſke me how Her diſpu-tation with ſathan.
I dare come to him for mercie, hee being a righteous God, ⁊ I a
miſerable ſinner? I tel thee ſathã, I am bold (through Chriſt) to

C 3   come

come vnto him, being assured and certaine of pardon & remission of al my sinnes for his names sake. For dooth not the Lord
bid all that bee heauie laden with the burden of sinne, to come
vnto him, and hee will ease them? Christes armes were spred
wide open (Sathan) vpon the Crosse, (with that shee spred her
owne armes) to imbrace me, and all penitent sinners: and therfore sathan, I will not feare to present my selfe before his
footstoole, in ful assurance of his mercy for Christ his sake. What
more? sathan, doost thou say it is written, that God will reward euerie one according to his desarts? So it is written a-
gaine (thou deceitefull Deuill) that Christes righteousnes, is
my righteousnesse, his workes my workes, his deserts my de-
desertes, his merrits my merrits, and his pretious
bloud a full satiffaction for all my sinnes. Oh but God is a iust
God thou sayest, and therfore must needes in iustice condemne
me. I graunt, sathan, that he is a iust God, and therefore he cannot in iustice punish me for my sinnes, which hee hath punished
alreadie in his owne Sonne. It is against the law of Iustice to
punish one fault twice. I was and am a great debter vnto God
the Father, but Christ Iesus hath paide the debt for me, & therefore it standeth not with the iustice of God to require it againe.
And therefore auoide Sathan, auoide thou firebrand of hell: a-
voide thou damned dog, and tempt me no more, for hee that is
with me is mightier than thou, euen the mightie and victorious
Lyon of the tribe of Iuda, who hath bruised thy head, & hath pro-
missed to be with his Children to the end of the world. Auoide
therefore thou dastard, auoide thou cowardly Souldiour, re-
mooue thy siedge, and yeeld the field won, and get thee packing,
or else I will call vpon my graund Captaine Christ Iesus, the
valiant Michael, who beate thee in heauen, & threw thee downe
to hell, with all thy hellish traine and deuilish crue. She had
scarcely pronounced these last wordes, but she fell suddenly into
a sweete smiling laughter, saying: now hee is gone, now hee is
gone, doe you not see him flie like a coward, & runne away like
a beaten Cocke? He hath lost the field, and I haue won the victorie, euen the Garland and Crowne of euerlasting life: and
that not by my owne power or strength, but by the power and
might of Iesus Christ, who hath sent his holye Angels to keepe
mee.

mee. And speaking to them which were by, she said, Oh would
God you saw but what I see. For beholde I see infinite mili-
ons of moste glorious angels stand about me, with fiery charets
readie to defend mee, as they did the good Prophet Elizeus.
These holy Angels, these ministring spirits, are appointed by
God to carry my soule into the kingdom of heané, where I shal
behold the Lord face to face, and shal see him not with other, but
with these same eyes. Now I am happy & blessed for euer, for I
haue fought the good fight, & by the might of Christ haue woone
the victory. Now from hence foorth I shal neuer taste, neither of
hunger nor colde, paine nor woe: miserie nor affliction, veratió
nor trouble, feare nor dread, nor any other calamity or aduersity
whatsoeuer. From hence foorth is laide vp for me a crowne of
life, which Christ shall giue to them which loue him. And as I
am now in possession thereof by hope, so shall I bee anon in full
fruition thereof by presence of my soule, and hereafter of my bodie also, when the Lord shall please. Then shee spake softly to her
selfe as followeth. Come Lord Iesus, come my loue Iesus, Oh
send thy Pursevant sweete Iesus to fetch mee. Oh sweet Iesus
strengthen thy seruant, and keepe thy promise. Then sang shee a
Psalme moste sweetly, and with a cheerefull voice: which done,
shee desired her husband that the 133. Psalme might be sung before her to Church. And further shee desired him that hee would
not mourne for her, aleadging the apostle Paul, where he saith:
Bretheren I would not haue you to mourne as men without
hope, for them that die in the Lord: affirming that she was not
in case to be mourned for, but rather to be reioyced of, for that
she should passe (shee said) from earth to heauen, from men to
holy angels, Cherubins, and Seraphins, to holy saints, Patri-
arkes and fathers : yea to God himselfe. After with wordes
veris suddainely she seemed as it were greately to reioyce, and
looke cheerefully, as though shee had seene some glorious sight:
and lifting vp her whole bodie, and stretching foorth both her
armes, as though shee would imbrace some glorious & pleasant
thing, said : I thanke my God through Iesus Christ he is come
he is come, my good Iaylor is come to let my soule out of prison.
O sweete death thou art welcome: welcome sweete death, neuer was there any guest so welcome to me as thou art: welcome
                                                                        the

Her guard
of Angels.

Her medi-
tation.

Her request
to her hus-
band not to
mourne for
her.

Her talke
with Death
and friendly
welcom-
ming of
him.

the messenger of euerlasting life: welcome the doore and entrance into euerlasting glorie, welcome I say &thrice welcome my good Jaylor, doe thy office quickly, and set my soule at libertie: Strike sweet death, strike my heart, I feare not thy stroke. Now it is doone: Father, into thy blessed hands I commend my spirit: sweet Iesus into thy hands I commend my spirit: blessed spirit of God, I commit my soule into thy hands. O moste holy, blessed and glorious Trinitie, three persons, and one true and euerlasting God, into thy blessed hands I commit my soule and my body. At which wordes her breath stayed, & so neither mouing hand nor foote, she slept sweetely in the Lord.

Her last wordes.

Her death.

Thus thou hast heard (gentle Reader) the discourse of the vertuous life, and Christian death of this blessed and faithfull Seruant of God, Mistresse Katherine Stubbes, which is so much the more wonderful, in that shee was but young & of tender yeres, not halfe a yere aboue the number of 20. when she departed this life. The Lord giue vs grace to follow her good example, that we may come to those vnspeakeable ioyes wherein shes now resteth through Christ our Lord, to whome with the Father and the holy Ghost, be all honour, praise, dominion & thankesgiuing, both now and for euermore.
Amen.

FINIS.
17 JY 60

The Confession and Conversion ... (*STC* 16610) is reproduced here, by permission, from the unique copy at The Huntington Library (RB 28356). The text block of the original measures 61 × 105 mm.

The blotted word on the title page reads HONO-RABLE

THE

CONFESSION
AND
CONVERSION

OF THE RIGHT HONO-
RABLE, MOST ILLVSTRI-
OVS, AND ELECT LADY,
MY LADY,

C. OF L

MATH. 22.

Yee erre, not knowing the Scriptures.

I. IOHN. 4.

Dearly beloved, belieue not euerie Spi-
rit, but try the Spirits, whither they be
of GOD, *for many false Prophets*
are gone out into this World.

EDINBVRGH
Printed by *John Wreittoun.* 1629.

A CONFESSION.

AS it was rare, vnexſpected, and long wiſhed for, of all that honored and loved her, ſo is it to be as ſeriouſly to be read, and conſcienciouſlie to bee conſidered of all, or ignorant and wilfull Papiſts of this land: Not ſo much in regard of her rank, perſon, and place, but rather in ſo farre, as that in that faith much beyond her ſexe, ſhe exceeded in knowledge more than many others who yet wilfullie and moſt ignorantlie ſtill continue in their error.

PSAL.

PSAL. 77.

MY voice came to GOD when I cryed; my voice came to GOD & he heard me. In the day of my trouble I fought the Lord, &c. my foule refufed comfort. I did think vpon GOD, and was troubled. I prayed, and my fpirit was full of anguifh. Thou keept mine eyes waking. I was aftonied, and could not fpeake. Pfal. 119. 81. My foule fainted for thy falvation; Yet will I waite for thy word. 82. Mine eyes faile for thy promife, faying, when wilt thou comfort me? 92. Except thy law had beene my delite, I fhould now haue perifhed in my affliction. I will never forget thy precepts, for by them thou haft quickued me. I am thine, faue me, for I haue fought thy precepts. 15. I will meditate therein, and confider thy wayes. 59. I haue confidered my owne wayes, and turned feate to thy teftimonies. 67. Before I was afflicted I went aftray, but now I keepe thy Word. 71. It is good for me that I haue beene afflicted, that I may
learne

learne thy statuts. 58. *By thy Comman-*
dement thou hast made me wiser than mine
enemies. I haue had more vnderstanding
than all my teachers, for thy testimonies are
my meditations. I vnderstood more than
the ancient, because I delighted in thy pre-
cepts. 104. *By thy precepts haue I gotten*
vnderstanding, therefore I hate all the
wayes of falshood. 29 *Now, take from*
me the way of lying, and grant me gra-
ciously thy law. 30. *I haue chosen the*
way of trueth, and thy iudgement haue I
layde before me. 173. *O Lord let thine*
hand helpe me, for I haue chosen thy pre-
cepts. 176. *I haue gone astray lyke a*
lost sheepe: seeke thy servant, &c. 103.
The entrance to thy Words sheweth light,
and giveth vnderstanding to the simple.
124. *Deale with thy servant according*
to thy mercie, and teach me thy statuts.
   74. *So they that feare thee, seeing*
    me, shall rejoyce, because
      I haue trusted in
       thy Word.

     A M E N.

              THE

THE CONVERSION AND CONFESSION OF THE RIGHT NOBLE C. OF L.

*O send out thy light, and thy trueth
let them lead mee, let them bring me
vnto thine holy hill, and to thy
Tabernacles. PSAL. 43.*

*I will heare what GOD the LORD will
speake, for hee will speake peace vnto
his people, and to his Saints; but
let them not turne againe vnto
follie. PSAL. 85. 8.*

I Perfitlie knowing, and fullelie assuring my soule, that there is no pos-
sibilitie of salvation to me, but alla-
nerly in the free mercie of GOD, and precious satisfaction of his Sonne my only
Saviour, who is able to saue them to the
vttermost that come vnto GOD by him,
seeing he ever liveth to make intercession
for them, *Heb.* 7. 25. neither is there salvation in any other, *Act.* 4. 12.

2. I renounce and condemne all wor-
shipping, or praying to Angels, hee or
shee

ſhe Saints, not now excepting the bleſſed Virgin *Marie*, and conforme to the
expreſſe direction of the Angell to Iohn.
Revel. I take me to worſhip GOD; and as
CHRIST, *Math.* 4. 10. commandeth
him only to ſerue, and to pray to my
father. *Math.* 8. 9. who is in Heaven,
to whom only belongeth religious worſhip, both of prayer and praiſe.

3. I renounce and condemne all prayers in Latin, or any vnknowne tongue
to mee, taking mee heereafter, by the
grace of GOD to pray with the Spirit,
and with vnderſtanding alſo, 1. *Cor.*
14. 15. and not to mumble and number my prayers according to the order
and diſtinction of beads, which I haue
cauſed breake and deſtroy, with preſent
and perpetuall thankſ-giving to GOD
therefore.

4. I acknowledge with *Ieremie* 10.
14. that a molten image is faiſhood,
they are vanitie and the workes of errors: and therefore caſting away all thoſe
abominations of images, pictures, me-
dalles, and pretended reliques; I take
mee

me whollie to the pure and plaine Gof-
pell of IESUS CHRIST, and his holie
Sacraments, wherein the lyuelie picture
of CHRIST is, and the moſt hallowed
Crucifixe that I can ſet before mine eyes,
handle with mine hands, or carrie vpon
my breaſt; wherein I rejoice, and euer
ſhall doe, by Gods helpe and aſſiſtance,
and finds great comfort in the conference
and prayers of GODS Miniſters, who
now reſort vnto me frequently: reſol-
ving by the grace of GOD never there-
after to craue, nor admit the company
and conference of Prieſts, and other teachers of lyes, guides of idolatrie; which
all now I haue forſaken by the light and
force of GODS Spirit: and woes mee
that I hearkned ſo long to theſe ſeducers.

5. I acknowldge that the bowing
downe before images is forbidden by
GODS Law, *Exod.* 20. 5. as well as
worſhipping of them. That images are
altogether bruttiſh and fooliſh , *Ierem.*
10. 3. I feare them not, for they can
doe no evill, neither is it in them to
doe good: but foraſmuch as there is none
like

like to thee O LORD, thou art great, &
thy Name is great in might: Who would
not feàre thee, O KING of Nations?
Ierem. 10. 5. 6. 7.

6. I embrace the holy Scriptures of the
old and new Testament, wherein is the
perfite rule of *faith* and *maners*, acknowledging that the writs and judgements of
all men should be tryed thereby, and re-
duced therevnto, or else altogether reje-
cted. And therefore I will curse & reject
and cast from me all blasphemous bookes
in write or print, (whereof alace I had
so many too long) contrare to GODS
trueth in these holy Scriptures.

7. I confesse and professe that the Scriptures are plaine and pure, being *a lampe
vnto my feete, and a light vnto my path,*
Psal. 119. 105. in all things necessare for
me to know my salvation. And seing
CHRISS commandeth vs *Ioh.* 5. 39. to
search the Scriptures, and the Bereans are
commended for searching the Scriptures
dayly, *Act.* 17. 11. I condemne the for-
bidding of their translations in vulgare
languages, and the reading of them by the
people.

people. And from my heart I deteſt that
ſaying, that ignorance is the mother of
devotion;bewailing my former ignorance
and ſtryving more and more to increſe
in all ſpirituall vnderſtanding.

8. With *Paul*. 1 *Tim*. 4. 3. I acknowledge the commanding to abſteine from
meates for conſcience ſake, to be from ſe-
ducing ſpirits, and doctrines of devils, for
the Kingdome of GOD is not meate and
drink, *but righteouſneſſe, peace, and joy
in the holy Ghoſt. Rom. 14. 17.* Neither
doth that *which entereth in at the mouth
defile a man, but that which proceedes out
of the mouth that defiles a man.*

9. I acknowledge and belieue. *Rom.* 3.
24. that I am juſtified freely by GODS
grace, through the redemption that is in
CHRIST IESUS, without any reſpect to
my workes; whereof I neither can, nor
ſhould boaſt with the proud Phariſee, but
with the penitent Publican. I cry to God
continuallie to be mercifull to me, who
am a miſerable ſinner, and with St. *Paul*.
the chiefe of ſinners, and ſo I belieue not
the ſatisfaction made by me, but the free
remiſſion

remission of fins, perſwading my ſelfe that *the wages of ſin is death, Rom* 6. 23. but the gift of GOD is eternall life, through CHRIST IESUS our LORD, and we his litle floke ſhould not feare, ſeing as our Saviour ſayeth, *Luke* 12. 32. *It is our Fathers pleaſure to giue vs a Kingdome,* which we could neuer merit by our ſelues, or any other creature for vs.

10. I acknowledge no fire after this life that purgeth vs from our fins, and temporall puniſhments, but as in *Ioh.* 1. 7. the blood of IESUS CHRIST his Son purgeth vs from all our fins, without any exception or deſtruction of fin what-ſoever, and as the ſoules of the wicked immediatly after death goe to hell, ſo the ſoules of the godly goe to Heaven.

11. I acknowledge and belieue with S^{t}. *Paul.* 1 *Cor.* 10. 16. that the Cup in the Lords Supper is not the blood, but figuratiuely the communion of his bodie. And with *Ioh.* 6. 30. The way how to eate and drink of this body is to belieue in him, and the Doctors, and Cannons of the Roman Church affirmeth the ſame
with

with vs, for the holy Scripture is full
of such maner of speaches; and our Saviour himselfe in this same place sayeth
that *Whosoever beleiveth in him shall not
thirst*, plainely making vs to vnderstand
that this thirst is quenched only by beleiving, and not by the drinking at the
mouth: and in *Ioh. 6. 56.* he sayeth,
*Whosoever eateth my flesh, and drinketh
my blood, abideth in me and I in him*:
and in verse 35. *Who comes vnto mee
shall not hunger*, and *who beleiveth in
mee shall never thirst*: So he eateth and
drinketh, who commeth vnto me, who
beleiveth in me, and abideth in mee.
and alitle after, having said, *Who beleiveth in me hath eternall life*, inferreth
thereby that he is the bread of lyfe.
Hee is then meate indeed, but for our
soules, not for our bodyes; which is to
be had by beleiving, not by swallowing.
And so expondeth *Origen* an ancient father, in his Hom. 12. in *Math.* this
same place. According to the Apostle
his exhortation, I am heartly desirous
after tryall of my selfe, 1. *Cor.* 11. 18.

olt

oft to eate of that bread, and drink of
that Cup, and fo (as praifed be GOD)
I latelie did rreeaue that holie Sacrament, publicklie in GODS Sanctuarie,
vnder both the kynds, for the food of
my foule, whereby now I find great
peace and comfort.

12 I acknowledge alfo, and beleiue,
that the Maffe is not a propitiatorie facrifice, but a blafphemous, and idola-
trous abomination, altogether deroga-
torie to CHRISTS propitiatorie facrifice, who once in the end of the world
to appeare, came to put away finne, by
that only one facrifice of himfelfe, and
who once was offered to beare the
finnes of many, *Heb.* 9. 26. 28. and
by that one offering, for ever hee hath
perfited all them that are fanctified,
Heb. 10. *v.* 14. 15.

13. I acknowledge, and beleiue,
that the Pope is not CHRISTS Vic-
care, nor Peters fucceffour, but hee is
that man of finne, the foune of perdition, and that verie great Antichrift de-
fcribed by St. *Paul,* 2. *Theff.* 2. Who
will

will judge all men, whether they bee
Kings or subjects, and bee judged of
none, and will haue all men vnder paine
of damnation to bee subject to him, as
their owne supreame Lord, both in spirituall and temporall things.

I did also before my conversion after
long tryall find some great oddes, and
verie remarkable differences betweene
the Pastors of the reformed Kirk, and
that of the Roman Kirk: And first that
the Pastors of the reformed Kirk would
bee judged by the word of GOD; but
the Pastors of the Roman Kirk would
be judges of the word of GOD.

2 The reformed Pastors would bee
ruled; but the Roman Kirk would bee
the rule themselues, saying, that the
Kirk is soueraigne judge of all doubts
of faith, and that it can not erre. And
so I perceaue in this question: If the
Roman Kirk may erre; or if it bee soueraigne and infallible judge, it must
bee that the Roman Kirk shall be judge,
and so consequentlie shee shall be both
judge and partie.

I haue also obserued this difference
betweene the two religions, which is,
that the reformed Kirk hath no rules
that teacheth vices: but the Roman Kirk
hath sundrie rules that teacheth men to
doe evill, and to disobey GOD. Such
is the rule of the councell of *Constance*,
that a man is not bound to keepe any
faith and truth to Hereticks. Such is
the doctrine, that the Pope may dispense
with the expresse Commandeme^t of
GOD, by dispensing with the Cup in
the Sacrament, by dispensing with othes
and vowes, in granting permission to
a man to man-sweare himselfe, neither
yet to performe any waves that which
wee haue promised to GOD. Such are
the disobedience of young infants towards their fathers and mothers, maintained & authorized by the Roman Kirk,
when a young childe is entred into a
closter contrare the will of his father.

Such are also the foundations of pub-
lick Bordels, whereby the Pope himselfe draweth great tribute.

Such are also the revolt of subjects
from

from their Prince, and againſt them, when it ſhall pleaſe the people to diſpenſe with their Oath of alledgeance, which they haue ſworne to their King.

I haue found alſo the plaine text of Scripture in many places moſt pittifully corrupted, and wrongouſly perverted by the Roman Kirk, and ſome I remarked moſt carefully, as followeth.

It is ſaid in the 2 Epiſt. to the *Hebrews* verſe 21. *That Iakob worſhipped GOD leaning vpon the end of his ſtaffe;* but the Byble of the Roman Kirk hath, *Iakob worſhipped the end of his ſtaffe,* thereby to eſtabliſh the adoration of Creatures.

The lyke corruption is in the Pſal. 99. *v.* 5. Where David ſayeth *Worſhippe towards his footſtoole:* the Roman Bible hath, *Worſhippe his footſtoole:* and in Geneſ. 3. *v.* 15. GOD ſaid, *The ſeede of the woman ſhould treade downe the head of the Serpent:* the Roman Kirk hath, *the woman ſhall bruiſe the head of the Serpent;* that is the Virgin Marie ſhall bruiſe downe the head, &c.

B   Againe

Againe in S^r. Pauls Epist. Rom. 11
6. is cutted off, two lynes being omit-
ted: For these are the words of the A-
postle, *But, if it bee of workes it is no
more of grace, or else were workes no
more workes,* which are left out in the
vulgare translation.

And where S^r. Peter sayeth, *Heere
are two swords:* the Roman Kirk most
ridiculouslie expoundeth thus, that the
Pope hath power over the spirituall and
temporall.

And where the Evangelist sayeth,
Doe this in rememberance of mee: the
Romish Church expoundeth thus, sacrifice my body in a sacrifice propitiatorie for the quick and the dead.

And another falshood I remember,
is, where our Saviour speaking of the
Cuppe in the Sacrament, sayeth, *This
Cuppe is the new Covenant in my blood
which is shed for you:* But the Bible of
the Romish Church hath into it, *This
Cuppe is the new Covenant in my blood,
which shall bee shed for you,* least a
man should perceaue that IESVS
CHRIST

CHRIST spake of a sacramentall shedding of his bloode: For as yet hee
had not then really shed his bloode
which hee had begunne to shed in his
passion.

These and many other falshoods did
I many tymes remarke, as they were
objected vnto me, yet did I ever mis-
regard them, being ever discontented
that any should speake to mee of such
hereticall opinions, (as I called them)
because my ghostly fathers assured mee
continually that it was a deadly sinne
any wayes to doubt, or to let it so
much as once enter into my thought,
that ever the Church might or could
erre, continually dinging in my eares a
warrant out of the Prophet *Malachie*;
cap. 2, verse 8. that the Preists cannot
erre, where it is thus read, *The Preists
lips shall keepe knowledge, and they shall
seeke the law at his mouth.*

This many yeeres contented mee,
till at last in my old dayes GOD so
happily moved my heart to heare the
trueth of better and sounder instructers,

and

and their warrand, (I praise GOD for
it) who sheweth to me that the words
of the Prophet are, and ought to bee
translated thus, yet men that are ledde
with an opinion that the Kirk cannot
erre will never consider this: *The Preists
lippes should keepe knowledge*: For they
that translate thus the words, and
*that they shall seeke the law at his
mouth*, they did never intend to shew
thereby, that GOD did make heere a
promise that so it shall bee for ever,
but onely to shew that this is the law
and commaadement of GOD, teaching
what the Preists and people should doe,
and onght to doe, even as in the Com-
mandement, *Thou shall haue no other
GODS but mee*: Now I find that the
words doe not promise that the Israelites should alwayes acknowledge and
worshippe IEHOVA the true GOD a-
lone, (for as may bee seene in the text
within fourtie dayes the event shewed
the contrarie) but shew what they ought
to doe, but the wordes are a Comman-
dement recited, not a promise made:
For

For the words of the fourth verse did show it: Therefore men not partially led may easily perceaue that the translation of the reformed Kirk is most perfect of all, showing not onely the sense and meaning of the law, but also how it did bind the people and Priest, and how they ought to obey it.

By this I thinke it no heresie, and I beleiue with the reformed Kirk that it is Gods holy trueth, that Preists succeeding in the place and office of *Aaron* and *Moses* may erre, and haue erred: yea, I thinke it the greatest error of all errors to thinke that a man can not erre, were hee neuer so holie. I perceaue now *Moses* Chayre in the which the *Scribes* and *Pharisees* did sit, was the seate wherein they were wont to read the law of *Moses*, and the expositions thereof to the people, for what they there did teach was true, and therefore C H R I S T commanded them to obey it. To sitte in *Moses* Chaire, I vnderstand, is to teach *Moses* doctrine, but (as the Iewes made

GODS

GODS law voyd by their owne glosses &
traditions) they erred most damnablie,
and were no more in *Moses* Chaire,
and so the people were no more bound
to obey it. For at that tyme CHRIST
himselfe called their doctrine sowre lea-
ven, and warned his Disciples to be-
ware of it.

I know also, and simelie now belieue, that it was never the purpose of
GODS Spirit in that place, or by these
wordes to teach, that the Law should
alwayes bee taught truelie and infalla-
blie by the Priests and Pastors, who
succeede *Moses* or the Apostles in the
Church by a continued succession: For
that is a falshoode con*rare to experience
in all ages: That this is most certaine,
I desire but any of a contrare opinion
to read but the same verie place with
an indifferent and vnprejudged minde,
which confutes it most evidently: For
in reading the same attentiuelie, *I* find
the Priests vnto whom the Prophet
there speaketh in these places, were
Levits, and directly succeeded *Aaron* in
the

the Preisthood: And yet yee see by the
plaine text they were departed out of
the way: they caused many fall in the
law by their corrupt glosse, and their
abuse of the Covenant of *Levi*, as it
appeareth most clearely into the next
words following immediatly: Yea, some
of them (yee see) had sacrificed to
Idolles, which I haue read my selfe in
Iosephus historie of these tymes, and
therefore the LORD threatneth to corrupt their seede by cutting off the male
progenie, and to cast the dung of their
sacrifices in their faces.

Finally I hope now in the mercie of
GOD yet before I die, to heare a hundreth sermons in GODS true Kirk: for
now my onely joy is my new birth,
that by the mercie of my GOD I am
regenerate, and of a daughter of darknesse and death that haue beene from
my naturall birth, am now made a
daughter of light and lyfe in my old
age, and my setled peace and comfort
is my spirituall marriage with my head
and

and husband the Lord Iesus Christ,
who hath marryed mee to himfelfe in
trueth and everlafting compaffion, and
will take from mee my old corrupt
garment, and clothe mee with the white
robe of his righteoufneffe, fo that my
nakedneffe fhall never appeare any more.

Now O Lord my God, and gracious Father in thy Christ, my
fweete Saviour, let thy Spirit quicken
mee more and more, thy wifdome guide
mee, thy grace fanctifie mee, and thy
Word inftruct me: Let the holy Ghoft
of whom thy Sonne my Saviour
was conceived, beget in mee, and mee
in thee, by the immortall feede of thy
Word: Let my faith conceaue, my repentance honour thee, my loue embrace thee, my zeale continuallie keepe
thee with mee, till the comming againe
of thy Sonne for my ever hoped glo-
rification: So come vnto mee Lord
Iesus, come quicklie, Amen.
*Bleffed be the Lord, for he hath fhew-
ed me his mercifull kindneffe. Pfal 31.21.*
Why

*Why art thou caſt downe my ſoule, and
why art thou diſquyeted within mee?
hope in GOD, for I ſhall yet praiſe
him, who is the hope of
my Salvation, and my
GOD. Pſal. 42. 11.*

PSALME. XLI. I.

I Waited patiently vpon the LORD, and hee inclyned vnto mee, and heard my cry. Hee brought mee alſo out of the horrible pit, out of the myrie clay, and ſet my ſeete vpon the Rocke, and ordered my goings. And hee hath put into my mouth a new ſong of Praiſe vnto our God. Many ſhall ſee it, and feare, and ſhall truſt into the LORD. Bleſſed is the man that maketh the LORD his truſt, and regardeth not the proud, nor ſuch as turne aſyde to lyes.

7. Then ſaid I, loe, I come, for in the roll of thy booke it is written of mee. I deſire to doe thy good will, O my GOD. Yea, thy law is within my heart, I haue declared thy righteouſneſſe in the great
congrega-

congregation: Loe, I will not refraine my lips, O LORD, thou knoweſt.

PSALME 86. 11.

Teach mee thy way, O LORD, and I will walke in thy trueth, knit my heart vnto thee, that I may feare thy Name.

17. *SheW a token of thy goodneſſe toward mee, that they Which hate mee, may ſee it, and bee aſhamed, becauſe thou LORD hath helped me, and conforted me.*

PSALME 116. 6.

The LORD preſerveth the ſimple, I Was in miſerie, and hee ſaved mee. Re-turne vnto thy reſt, O my ſoule, for the LORD hath béene beneficiall vnto thee.

PSALME 109. 26.

Helpe mee O LORD my GOD, ſaue mee according to thy mercie, and they ſhall know that this is thy hand, and that thou LORD haſt done it. If the LORD had not helped mee, my ſoule had almoſt dWelt in ſilence.

PSALME 101.

Mine eyes ſhall bee vnto the faith-full of the Land, that they may dWell With mee: Hee that Walketh in a perſite

Way

way shall serue mee, there shall no de-
ceatfull person dwell in mine house, neither shall hee that telleth lyes remaine
in my sight.

PSALME. 56. 12.

I will now render praise vnto thee,
13 For thou hast delyvered my soule
from death, and my feete frm falling,
that I may walke before GOD in the
light of the living.

PSALME 103.

Blessed bee the Name of the
LORD from hencefoorth
and for ever,
AMEN.

A PRAYER.

PSAL. 45.

10 Hearken (O daughter) and consider,
encline thine eare, forget also thine owne
people, and fathers house.

AS thou O LORD art great and
wonderfull in all thy workes: yet
thy mercie shineth above all thinges:
Albeit

Albeit I forſooke thee O LORD, yet thou
haſt not forſaken mee: I haue turned my
back to thee, yet thou calleſt mee thy
Childe: All that thou requireſt at mine
hands is, that I would hearken vnto thee.
And why ſhould I not hearken vnto thee,
ſith that all our deſtruction came from
thence, that our fathers turned their eares
from thee, to liſten vnto the voice of the
ſlie and ſubtile Serpent? Grant me grace
that I may haue a willing and obedient
heart, that by the meanes of good foode,
that ſhall receaue in thy Word, which
alace too long I haue forſaken, I may forget my wicked nature, originall ſin, and
all the vices which I did bring with mee
from my mothers wombe; that I forget
the world, to giue my ſelfe wholly vnto
thee, and thy ſervice; that I forget mine
owne workes, and mine owne opinions,
to depend wholly on thy grace. And if the
Bride, and new married woman forſake,
and leaue her fathers houſe to follow her
husband: if ſhe leaue the ſport and paſtime
of her youth, to goe about her houſwiſrie,
and to conforme her ſelfe vnto her huſband :

band: why fhould not I alas! forfake that
which difpleafeth thee, to be agreeable
vnto thy Son IESUS CHRIST, which in
fo great mercie hath wedded me? And albeit I was a ftraunger from his league, &
promifes of everlafting lyfe, notwithftan-
ding he hath joyned himfelfe vnto me in
hearty loue, & ratified his league with his
precious blood. Let me therefore O Lord
be as his chaft and faithfull fpoufe, and let
me be obedient vnto the will of our good
LORD, which doth me this honour to
place me by his fide, and to take mee not
only for his *fervant*, but alfo for his *child*,
his *friend, his deare and welbeloved Sponfe,*
Ioh. 15. Grant me O LORD that I follow
no more ftrange Gods to delight in them,
but that my loue and affection be wholly
fet on him. I will therefore endevour my
felfe to pleafe him. I will loue him, and
loue that which he loveth. I will honour
him, fith he hath fo much honoured mee.
I will forfake all things to follow him, fee
ing he forfooke the Heavens to faue mee
on earth. O happie marriage! Of the marriage of Adam and Eue came fo many vn-
thrifts,

thrifts, so many wretches, and miserable
catiues, bond-slaues to Sathan, and of
their owne nature, detestable and abho-
minable before the face of GOD. But of
this holy marriage, are new borne, the
elect, the vessels of glorie, the children of
GOD, the heires of euerlasting lyse: whom
GOD so loveth and esteemeth, taking
pleasure in their beautie, wherewith he
doth adorne and deck them through his
Son CHRIST IESUS: which gifts LORD
make me partaker thereof, and let the
praise be ascribed vnto thee, for that great
and glorious light of thy Word, showne
vnto me, from henceforth and for ever,
AMEN.

THis profession of faith, meditaci-
ens, prayers, and prayses, as they
were most joyfullie; and constantlie
vttered, and declared before many honorable men and women: So were they
most heartilie sealed and subscryued
by the right religious, most
noble, and truely wise La-
die, the 25. of Maij.
FINIS.

The Conflict in Conscience … (*STC* 16661) is reproduced here, by permission, from the British Library copy, Shelfmark 4920.aa.49. The text block of the original measures 110 mm from 1st line to final line (B3r).

The blotted lines on the title page read:

her Pastor and her at diverse times.

THE
CONFLICT IN
CONSCIENCE OF A
deare CHRISTIAN, named
BESSIE CLARKSONN
in the Parish of Lanerk,
Which shee lay vnder
three yeare & an half.

With the conference that past betWixt her Pastor and her
at

Newly corrected and amended.

EDINBVRGH
Printed by Iohn Wreittoun. 1632.

To the Christian Reader.

His conference (Christian Reader) came foorth at the first by my knowledge. I found the words of this deare defunct of greater worth than that they should fall to the ground, and not to bee gathered: so at last, as I visit I wrote, but not to put out to the view of the World: yet some hath done it by an uncorrect coppie, wherein my words are made hers at sometimes, and hers mine. Wherefore at the desire of the Printer and other good people I haue given a just coppie, intreating heartily the Almightie, that you who reads it may make profitable vse of it to his glorie, and thy owne everlasting good.

Thine in the LORD
W. L.

A 2   THE

The conflict in confcience of a
deare Chriftian, named *Beffie
Clerkfone in the Parifh of
LANERK, which fhee lay*
vnder three yeare and
an halfe.

Minifter.

BESSIE *how are you?*
Beffie.
  I finde the wrath of an angrie
GOD, of a crabbed GOD; and all the
wrath that you preached, which come
on mee now: I finde him dayly comming againft mee.
  Min. *Beffie, GOD will for good ends*
let his owne deare children tafte of his
anger, and wreftle with his wrath in this
world, that they be not caften vp in a dead
fleepe of flefhly fecuritie; and fo perifh with
the wicked of the world, in that great
wrath that is to bee revealed; and to bring
them to an hatred of finne and forrow for
it: and to teach them how farre they are

  A 3   *obliged*

obliged to the Sonne of *GOD, who hath for them vndergone the full weight of that wrath, (for your trouble is but a sparke of that fire wherein Christ was burnt vp in a sacrifice to the Father) and that your hearts being racked with terrour, we may bee made for the greater peace, and the calme after the tempest may bee the sweeter when it comes, and Gods glorie the greater, and more manifest in that dealing, in casting downe, and plunging in the hell, and heauing againe to the heauens, & this sort of dealing drives atheisme best out of the heart.*

Bes. I am not a devill to contemne God, and I cannot get faith to belieue in God.

Min. It is a degree of faith to finde the want of faith, it is a step to a greater grouth.

When I was about to comfort her, shee said, Will yee speake to mee as yee should, and say, thou wretched, sinfull, and wicked woman, and not tell mee sweete words.

I answered her, No Bessie, I must not measure you as yee doe your self by your owne sense, but to teach you to hope a-
boue

boue hope; and say with Iob, *Lord, if thou will slay mee I will trust in thee?*

Bes. O there was grace there, but there is a great dissension betwixt God and mee; I am cast away; O that this awakning had come twenty yeares since! but now my time is lost; many come to Word and Sacrament that knowes not what they are doing; the morne when Gods people come to heare you I cannot come, I am cast aside.

Min. It is yet the acceptable time wherin the Lord may bee found, hee is yet on the throne of grace; giue no place to such suggestions of Sathan, and distrustfull cogitations, arysing of your corruption; and where yee cannot come to the Word, that is not to be laid to your charge: It is not an argument of Gods anger, when one by sicknesse, or trouble is with-holden who would faine bee there: but seeke you by prayer to God, who by his Spirit will teach you inwardly, and supply the want of the meanes by an inward working.

When I preassed to perswade her, that God in his owne time would ease her, and speake peace to her, I cannot

finde that, said she. Min. Albeit ye feele
it not, pray that the Lord would *remem-*
ber mercy in wrath, as the Prophet Hab.
3. 2. Mercy in wrath, said shee, O that
is a strange word! O for absolution! O
for a drop to coole my tormented soule!
O that I could win a step nearer him.

Min. Blessed are they that hunger &
thirst, for they shall bee satisfied. *It is*
the Lord who is our sufficiencie, who works
the will and the deed: it is hee who wakens
those desires in you, and hee will worke the
worke.

When I said the Lord delt with her
as hee doth, to humble her: To humble
mee, said shee, and that I am, that Catte
that sits there is in better case nor I am:
I shall beate downe this carcase with
beire-bread and water, but that doth not
the turne. When her servant woman said
you were a good body, and beginne to
commend her.

Cease, said shee, I am but a dog, and
worse nor a dog; Gods wrath is on me,
for my invisible sinnes, and if I were a-
way, there would be none but Christians
on the earth: I know Christ would goe
be-

betwixt mee and all my sinnes, but one,
I will not laine it, nor hyde it, it is despaire.

Min. *You are very sensible of your vn-*
beliefe, and God will make you also sensible
of a liuely faith or all bee done: for a litle
while hath hee forsaken you, as hee saith,
Isa. 54. 7. 8. 9. 10. but with great com-
passion will hee gather you: for a moment
in his anger, hath hee hid his face from
you for a little season, but with everlasting
mercy will hee haue compassion on you, I-
bid. 10. 11 O thou afflicted and tossed
with tempest! &c.

Bes. Is it God that doth this to mee.
Can God spoyle himselfe? I had faith and
prayer, now they are rest, couped and
spoyled: can God doe it? will God rob
himselfe? will hee take away the matter
of his owne glorie? I am ashamed to
looke any man in the face: I haue lost
the favour of God & man. O for a drop
of grace! O for *as much faith as a graine*
of mustard seede!

Min. Bessie *it is the Lord who deales*
with you, but not to rob your faith which
is his gift, and once given, commeth never

A 5   in-

*under revocation: Yet it continueth not
ay in alyke vigour and strength, but will
oft come under a great eclypse, and bee
brangled with doubtings, and shaking with
feares, for there is no perfection heere, and
all this exercise is to adde strength, that
yee wrestling with God as Iaakob did, may
prevaile in end; and that it is not lost, your
earnest desire evidently declareth.* And
when I shew her that wee walked by
faith and not by feeling, and must not
measure our selues, nor Gods goodnesse
and loue by our sense. Shee answereth,
if faith doe it not, I haue done with it.

When one beside spake to her of Gods
favour and presence. Shee said, God if I
were as sure of it as you are, I haue feete,
(said shee) hands, eyes, knees, I can doe
any thing but one, I cannot belieue, well
were the soule that euer it was ordained
that had faith: O the great want of faith
and loue to God in these dayes. It was
never lesse, and they will finde one day
what it is to want it: one thing holds
mee from God, it is vnbeliefe, G o d s
hand is sore on mee: I would faine belieue: Pray, pray, pray, (said shee) yee
that haue faith.   Min.

Min. The LORD *who* will not breake the bruised reede, nor quench the smoaking flaxe, *will bring your desire, and those weake beginnings to a greater grouth and perfection: for faith groweth by degrees, as that blind mans sight* Mark. 8. 24, 25.

When I told her of GODS dealing with his owne by diverse sorts of trouble in minde, body, and estate. Shee answereth, No trouble to the trouble in mind. I care not, said shee, for legges, armes, eyes, and all the rest, if I could get comfort in the blood of Iesus: I would not care my carcase lay lame, leper, sick, sore, so that my minde were pacified, and at one with God: I care not for all Sathans assaults if hee were even standing there so that I could finde God with mee, and not against mee.

Waite on, said I, the Lord will come, Shee answereth, Hee commeth daylie in wrath. But hee will come in mercie, said I, in his owne time, She answereth, Ever since this bred in me you said that, but I can never find it, would I willingly losse my soule, if I could get faith? well is the soule that ever it was ordained of

God,

God, that gets the comforts of the holy
Ghost.

Min *Would you not Beſſie bee one of his,*
Wallie, wallie, ſaid ſhe, to be one of his,
to haue one drop of grace from his finger end, who would not bee one of his?

Then, ſaid I, bleſſed are yee, for *bleſ-*
ſed are they that hunger and thirſt for
righteouſneſſe, for they ſhall bee ſatisfied.
Bleſſed are they that ſeeke in ſinceritie,
to bee one of that ſocietie of the Sainᵈts
of God, to haue the comforts of that
communion and priviledge of his people, for *bleſſed,* Pſal. 33. 12. *are theſe*
people whoſe God is the LORD, even the
people whom hee hath choſen for his owne
inheritance. And after I had prayed for
her, and preaſſed by ſome paſſages of
Scripture to comfort her. Shee ſaid, It
is heavy to my hart to heare thoſe ſweet
admonitions and prayers, and to get no
part of them in my ſoule, and not to find
him whom you ſeeke.

She ſayeth againe, Whether ſhall I
turne? Whether ſhall I goe? What ſhal
I doe? Whether ſhall I runne to ſeeke
God to grip him? I cannot get grippes
faſtned

faſtned on him. Deare Miniſter, ſaid ſhe, tell mee what ſinne hath procured this? that I am ſuch a ſpectacle to the world by all others? Heard you, reade you, knew you ever one like mee? Then I ſhew her of *Iob, Ieremie, David, Heze-kiah,* and others. And albeit *Beſſie* to your feeling yee cannot get grips faſtned on him, yet aſſuredly hee hath grippes faſtned on you; the good ſheepe-heard hath you in his hand & none ſhal plucke you out of it.

Beſ. I thinke, if ever I had had faith I could not haue loſt it. I anſwered, You haue not loſt it; you deſire, which GOD reputs for faith, and hath the ſame pro-miſe of ſatisfaction which ſaith hath made vnto it. She anſwereth, I would bee burnt quicke to be ſure of ſalvation: I liue without faith, I liue and worſhip not God, I can finde no comfort from God nor man; my life is miſerable and comfortleſſe.

Min. *That is even* Iobs *complaint, ſaid I,* Iob 3. 20. 21. *So albeit yee bee com-fortleſſe to your ſenſe; yet yee are not mar-vowleſſe, and hath the Saincts ſubject to*
the

the same tentation and tribulation with
you: and yee shall get in the Lords mercie
a blessed outgate with them: yea, although
wee bee never Witnesse to it, yet yee your
selfe shall feele it.

Bes. I am the most miserable and
wretched creature in the world, for my
sinnes are hid to my selfe, and knowne to
God.

Min. Bessie, God is not ay persuing
sinne When the soules of his Saints are per-
plexed and persued With horrours: Hee
seeth no iniquitie in Iaakob, nor sinne
in Israel: *albeit it setteth vs to seeke them*
out: and to sorrow for them: hee hath o-
ther ends wherefore he dealeth so with his
owne: namely, that hee may shew his worke
and glorifie his Name, as Christ *sayeth of*
that blind man. Iohn 9. 3.

After I had prayed, she said, if your
prayers haue a good ground and bee according to Gods will, its the better, it
wiil bee the better heard. But that it is,
said I, I haue a warrand to mourne with
them that mourne: and to pittie and
pray for all that are in trouble, chiefly of
my owne flocke: Your warrand were
the

the better, said shee, if I were one of
Chrifts flocke: happie were that foule
that were one of those. But yee are one
of these, said I. Yee haue aye said that
said shee, but I can never finde it. You
will finde it, said I, in the Lords time:
tarrie his leasure, hee will come with
comfort. Tarrie must I, said she, where
shall I flee or slit: hee commeth aye in
due time, but hee commeth to mee in
wrath. When I remembred her againe
of *Iob*, who said, *if thou wilt slay mee, I
will belieue in thee*. She answereth, where
will yee get the like of *Iob*; no, not a-
mongst you all that are Minifters: faithfull was hee, but I haue none; no salvation for mee. Then to trye her, I said,
will yee sell mee your part of it, your
title, right and kyndnesse; what shall I
giue you for it; if you haue none you may
the better cheape quite it, and I will
giue you for it. Shee answereth, Why
scorne yee mee, a filly poore woman, &
yee a wise man; I would buy and not
fell, if I had ten thousand millions of
gold, if I had a thousand worlds, if
it were to be bought for money, I wold
                                       giue

gine you all for it.

Min. *I said not this to scorne you Bessie,*
but to draw out your desire by this demand
as it doth: Whereby it is easie to discerne
that ye haue a sure title to that salvation,
albeit it seeme tint to your sence.

Bes. I haue no pleasure in any thing,
neither in husband nor childe: I can doe
nothing but sinne; my life is all sinne,
and it were to peale the barke of a kaile
castock and eate, I sinne in the doing of
it: why liue I then? *I* can not die, said
shee, *I* cannot liue, they will burie a carcase, will they burie mee, a carcase of
sinne: yea sinne it selfe.

When *I* speared at her, if shee desired
mercy. Shee answered, O that his desire to me, were as great as mine to him!
O for a looke of loue! Cry and pray,
said *I*, for the Lord hath said, *Seeke and*
yee shall finde: knocke and it shall be opned
vnto you. My prayer, said shee, is repel-
led: my cry is not respected: it doth no
good: *I* cannot haue faith, except God
giue it; none hath any grace but from
him; happie are they that can blesse him
and call on his name,

Min.

Min. *And happie are they Beſſie that*
counts them happie, and would with all
their heart be of that number as ye would.

Beſ. That ſtone in the wall hath as
great appetite to any bodily comfort of
meate, drinke, cloaths, or ſuch lyke as
I haue, for *I* cannot get the comforts of
the holy Spirit.

When *I* prayed for that conſolation
to her, that ſolide comfort which is
ſtronger nor tentation, tribulation, or
death it ſelſe. Shee ſaid, Why ware yee
your prayers on ſuch a vyle wretch?
God hath counted the number, and gathered them, and *I* am one moe. *I* will
not belieue you, ſaid *I*, Beſſie, albeit you
belieue the ſuggeſtions of *Sathan* in
your falſe heart: it is otherwiſe in the
accoumpt of God, and *I* will pray for
you that it may bee reuealed to you, and
pray yee with mee. And after *I* had
prayed, ſhee ſaid, Sayings will not doe
it, you doe your part, but if God worke
not, and he giue not, *I* cannot haue comfort. Can any haue grace till God giue
it? Can that ſtone belieue? Yet Beſſie,
ſaid *I*, let vs vſe the meanes and doe according

cording to Gods direction in his word,
and waite on till he who hath wounded
heale againe, and hee will make light a-
rife in the midst of your darknesse, the
light of consolation in the darknesse of
perturbation, and calme the tempest that
is in your conscience.

Bes. There is no friend to that soule
that is vnder Gods feede: I am vnder
Gods feede: and my husband, children,
nor no other are friends to mee, nay not
my selfe is a friend to my selfe: as for my
corps, I care not it were casten vp to
the heaven, and kepped on yron graps,
so my soule had peace.

*Min. Bessie, many hath peace with
themselues that hath none with GOD, as
secure sinners sleeping in sinne, and crying
peace: and some hath peace with God that
hath none with themselues; and as many
haue not the grace and faith, which they
thinke they haue, so some haue the grace
and faith which they thinke they haue not*

Bes. I care not my owne damnation,
if G o d bee glorified: what recke of
mee if hee get his owne gloric?

Min. *Bessie, assure your selfe these are*
not

riot the *Wishes and words of a castaway:*
and Gods glorie bee deare to you, you and
your salvation are deare to him.

When I speared if shee tooke meate
to refresh her bodie, Shee answered,
No, all craues that, both faithfull and
vnfaithfull, albeit the vnfaithfull be vn-
worthie of it, for they cannot glorifie
that God who giues it.

When I desired her to pray. Shee
answered, I haue no warrand, and hath
many letts. Will you say, said I, God
be mercyfull to me for Iesus sake. Shee
said, God bee mercifull to mee for thy
owne sake, for Christ hath not redeemed
all. Bessie, said I, yee must seeke in the
Name of IESVS, whom the father hath
sealed, in whom alone hee is reconciled
with vs, and for whose sake hee giveth
grace and mercie: lay your coumpt you
will never come to the Father but by
him..

Min. *Bessie. doe yee not pray when yee
are alone.* Shee answered, I will not
commend my selfe. When one pairt-
ing with her, said, God bee with you
Bessie. Shee answered, God forbid hee
were

were with you as hee is with mee. O
there is a great change comming, a feare
full alteration, a cuppe of wrath comming, wee are conceived and borne in
sinne, and what shall bee the end of sin.

Min. *Indeed Bessie sinne hath feare-*
full effects, but blessed bee that Sonne of
God Iesus, Who saveth his people frm their
sinne: there is no condemnation to them
that are in Christ.

Bes. *I* know if the devill were
chained there beside mee, hee cannot
without Gods permission hurt an haire
of mine head: but G o d beeing angry
with mee, hee turnes him louse and all
his instruments against me.

Min. *Bessie, the Lord loused him v-*
pon Iob: but so many linkes onely, that hee
Wan to his goods, children, body, but not
to his life, farre lesse to his soule: the Lord
will not give the soule of his Turtle to
the beast: the good Sheepe-heard hath
you in his hand, and none shall plucke
you out of it: *What ever be your feares,*
doubtings, or apprehensions vnder your
tryall, and present desertion

When some stan ding by spake to her,
shee

shee sayes, Take all that to your selfe
that yee say to me, yee haue no borrows,
no assurance more nor *I*, and knowes
not but yee may come in the lyke cace.

Min. *Indeed wee should take our war-*
ning by you, and wee haue all mister to ga-
ther and lay vp against the houre of tenta-
tion. I comming to her sayes, Bessie, Haue
yee gotten any comfort yet. Shee answered, When God sends it, I will get it.

But seeke yee it not, said I. She answereth, What availeth words when there
is nothing within. When *I* was blessing the Lord, shee doubled the word,
and said, Blessed bee hee, Blessed be he:
O that *I* could glorifie him! O
that *I* could get gripes fastned on him.
I see Bessie, said I, albeit you pray not,
yet you praise and blesse God. I cannot,
said shee, blesse him, hee is blessed in
himselfe: and I never heard him blasphemed, but I was grieved at it, I had rather
haue heard the evill spirit named ten
times, nor him once blasphemed, sye on
them that cannot blesse, and yet will
blaspheme him.

When I earnestly prayed for her, She
said, Why take yee paines on such a vile
wretched crea-

creature. I would Beſſie, ſaid I, haue
God glorifying himſelfe, in ſaving a loſt
ſoule, and magnifying his mercie on you,
who is miſerable. *I*, ſaid ſhee, that is
right good, God grant it, God grant it.
O there is little faith in the earth! and
loue is growne cold.

When *I* deſired her to pray and ſaid,
Long ſince Beſſie yee would haue prayed, why inſiſt yee not. Shee anſwered,
I had the will of prayer, but who hath
the ſpirit of prayer, God knowes: well
is the ſoule that is in Chriſt: but they
that are founded on that old father A-
dam, fearefull is their eſtate.

When *I* was poſing her with ſome
queſtions, about her inward eſtate. She
ſaid, Why examine yee mee ſo ſore, yet
vſe a ſharpe examination, and yet yee
will not bee my judge. Beſſie, ſaid *I*,
I would know your conſtitution, that *I*
may the better know how to deale with
you, *I* am about to inſtruct and comfort you, to vſe the meanes, and beg a
bleſſing from God vpon them, and *I*
haue ſeene when yee were better content that *I* conferred with you and pray-

ed for you. Shee answered, *It is a token*
that I get small comfort by them, The
Lord, said I, Bessie hath that to giue, hee
hath not cosredit the dispesatio of a dram
weight of grace to man nor Angell, hee
keepeth that in his owne hand, and dispen-
ses when & to whom, and after what measure & maner he pleases. But I see the devill in your corruption, not content that the
meanes be vsed. She answered, I find the
devill, the world, & the flesh fighting a-
gainst me, I feele, both satans assaults, and
I lye vnder Gods wrath, also which is
a fearefull cace, what recke of all sathans
assaults, if I lay not vnder Gods wrath.

Min. *The greater battell Bessie the*
greater victorie: I see a great conflict in
you and you your selfe findes it as you con-
fesse; yet happie are yee who are pursued
by sathan, and not possest by him and vn-
der peace with him. The LORD hath
divided betwixt you and him and drawne
you to that side whereon the seede of the
woman is; I finde faith fighting in you a-
gainst vnbeliefe, and where faith and vn-
beliefe are in one soule fighting, faith shall
ever prevaile, By faith is our victorie?
                                        1. Iohn

1. Iohn.5,4 *And what is the condition*
of the Christian euer after his calling, but
to feele this troublesome conflict, betwixt
nature and grace, spirit and flesh, the old
man and the new. But blessed bee GOD
Who shall trade sathan vnder our feete: so
albeit this battell bee burndensome, yet let
this beare you vp, that the LORD in end
shall giue you the victorie over all your e-
nemies. It were, said shee, a great comfort to mee, if *I* were perswaded of it:
but *I* cannot bee quite of infidelitie and
despaire: Well is the soule that ever it
came in the world, that can bee freed
of vnbeliefe, and gets grace to belieue
Lord banish the deuill and *I* shall belieue.

And some gentle-men, and others being with mee, shee directs her speach to
them, saying, Yee Gentle-men and simple, and all, Let my casting backe bee
your forward comming: well are yee
that can belieue and pray, but I haue
none: I haue no wit in the world, either
to blesse God or benefite my selfe; many
thousands get grace and faith, and I
would as faine haue it as any of them.

MIN.

MIN. Beſſie GOD meaſureth his owne by their vnfained deſire, and what you would bee in an heartie affeſtion, that you are in the accompt of God, and that ſecret ſeed of grace, which in this exerciſe vnder the aſhes of your corruption lyeth hidde, & dead as it were like ſeed in the ground, or hotte coales vnder aſhes, ſhall heereafter in the mercie of God budde and breake foorth, for it maye bee diſcerned alreadie in theſe divine deſires in your eſtimation of the bleſſedneſſe of thoſe that believs, & affeſtion to bee on that number.

MIN. Beſſie, is there any comfort coms et? Shee anſwereth, if it were come it would kyth, it would bud foorth: Oſt and many a time haue you ſaid comfort was comming, but I cannot finde it: alace, I am an outlaw to GOD, I weepe in the night when I ſhould ſleepe; I mourne when others are merrie; I am bound when they ate free; I haue a long-ſome laire, a feareſull & ſore laire heere: when others goe vp and downe, to and froe, I am a wonder to the world, and I am worthie to bee ſo.

Min. Beſſie, long delay is not an argu-

B   ment

ment of vtter denyall, & where yee mourne
where others are merrie, it is better to goe
to the house of mourning nor of feasting:
Blessed are they that mourne, saith Christ,
but woe to them that laugh. We are heere
in the vally of teares and kingdome of patience. The Lord will wype the teares
from your eyes, hee is leading you by hell to
heauen, and through many tribulations
and afflictions to his kingdome, peace shal
bee the end of your battels, and rest the
end of trouble. Wee haue Bessie brough
you a drinke of wine to comfort your spirit.
Wine, said shee, the worst water in the
Well is ouer good for mee, I will haue
no wine, why should I haue the benefite when it is neither blessed to me, neither can I blesse him that giues it. I care
not for outward bodily comforts, since
I cannot get the inward and spirituall.

 Min. Will yee seeke it of GOD Bessie
in the name of IESVS. Lord if thou wilt
said shee, the Lord hath power enough
but not finding faith in Iesus, shee said
shee wanted a warrand to seeke in his
Name. Min. I will shew you a warrant
Bessie, his owne command with a promise

50. *Pfal.* 15. *In the day of thy trouble,*
&c. 1. *Iohn.* 3.23. *This is his comman-*
dement that wee belieue, &c. Alſo hee
calleth, Math. 11. *on the wearie and*
laden, promiſing to eaſe them: you cannot
deny but you are both laden and wearie
vnder the loade. Therfore you are called
on, and the more miſerable you are, you
are the meeter object for mercy to worke
on: will you fly from the Saviour, becauſe
you are loſt, or from the Phyſitian, becauſe
you are ſicke. Alace, ſaid ſhee, *I* cannot
finde a warrand, *I* finde a wrong warrand. *What call you a wrong warrand,*
ſaid I. I cannot finde Chriſt, ſaid ſhee,
and any thing beſide him is wrong.
Min. But ſay, IESVS interceid for mee.
I will not blaſpheme him, ſaid ſhee, nor
bee a lyar, *I* am a lyar great enough already, for to mee to ſpeake the words
with my mouth without faith in my
heart, what is that but to take his name
in vaine.

Min. *Shall I pray for you Beſſie.*
What good, ſaid ſhee, can *I* get by your
prayers, except *I* had a heart to pray for
my ſelfe, *I* haue many things to ſeeke, if

I could get faith to belieue, and reliefe
to my spirit, and what matter of sawes
then: when I see that I saw not, then
shall I doe that I did not. These three
yeare I had not a faithfull desire, indeed
I thought it came all from your owne
mouth, all the inlacke of my prayers.

Min, *Howso Bessie, what heard you
mee say*. That prayers availed not, said
shee. Min. *I haue oft complained of our
prayers, as I had iust cause, and that God
might bee angrie against them, Psal 81.9.
and might repell them if he delt in iustice
with vs, but this was not to make vs leaue
off prayers, but to repent and pray more
feruently.*

*But the time hath beene when you de-
lighted in prayer, said I.* Shee answered,
I found comfort then in prayer. *I* had
no comfort but in prayer, *I* had many
calamities, and whom to should *I* seeke
but to God, and oft went *I* to him with
a grieued heart: had one God, what reck
of all the world, what recke who bee a-
gainst them if hee bee with them: but if
a soule bee vnder Gods seede, what a-
vaileth friends, kin, jewels, and all the
world.

world: Oh and alas for ever! that I
should want that blessing of his favour,
which hee bestowes on so many: Alace,
I haue gotten the poore mans answere,
you will not bee served.

Min. *Take not that answere Bessie:*
continue crying and knocking, for he hath
said, seeke and you shall finde: and that
poore Woman of Canaan, *that would not*
take a repulse, or nay-say, was satisfied in
end But I am none of his, said shee.
Bessie, said I, who told you that? the devill
would haue you thinke so: and will you take
his testimonie against you, who is a lyar
from the beginning, and not the witnesse of
the veritie, and Word of GOD *with you:*
beleeue not Sathan *nor your owne false*
heart, I know GOD *in his owne time will*
giue you comfort .

Bessie. The knowledg is yours, said she,
but the sorrow is mine: well is the soule
that getteth the holy Spirit, to seeke
grace and mercy at his hands: well is the
soule that getteth the benefite and the
blessing with it: but fye on them that
coumpts the sore afore the glorie, the
sore of the earth before the glory of hea-

B 3   ven

ven, it is no fore to them but a fearefull
curfe: Alace, I haue long to liue, and a
wretched life; I wearie vp, and I weary
downe, fighs helpe not, fobs helpe not,
groanes helpe not, and prayer is faint:
it is a fearefull calamitie, to haue woe
heere, and woe heereafter, to haue hell
heere, and hell heereafter for ever: the
matter is the leffe, they that gets a light
life, a lightfome life, that they get woe
heereafter; and a lightfome life is the
faith that many hath: but it is moft wofull and doolefull, to haue woe heere,
and woe heereafter for ever. *I* will tell
you my teftament, I haue beene in hell
thefe many yeares, and I looke never for
another heaven. O wretch that I am!
alace for ever, there a great flie cóming,
a fearefull cup, and I will get my fhare
of it, and it is nothing I feele heere, to
that that I feare for ever.

Min. *Beffie, the LORD corredts you
heere, that you perifh not with the world
for ever: hee woundeth and hee will heale
againe, albeit you can neither thinke it
nor feele it, nor hope for it, yet in his Name
I will affure you in his owne time hee will*

eafe

eafe you and ſpeake peace to you. I cannot, ſaid ſhee, find you a good ſpay-man
*Min. Yet if ever Beſſie I ſpake trueth, you
Will finde it: I promiſe you in the Name of
the LORD*. Shee anſwered, The Lords
Leivetennant will bee loath to lye; well
is his Lievetennant. *Whom call you ſaid
I, his Lievetennant*. You, ſaid ſhee, and
ſuch as you, yee are Tennants and not
maſters. Min. *Beſſie, grippe to the pro-
miſe of mercy, hope aboue hope*. I haue
not, ſaid ſhee, that gift of my ſelfe, if
God giue mee it not. *Seeke it of GOD*,
ſaid I, What recke of words, ſaid ſhe,
ſince I cannot get mends to my inward
parts. *I am ſure, ſaid I, if you ſhould goe
to hell Beſſie, you would goe to hell with
loue to GOD*. Shee anſwered, What
recke of my loue to him, ſince hee hath
none to mee, if hee had loue to mee, all
were well. Min. *But he loues you Beſſie, before you love him, for your loue is
the effect of his, and they whom hee loveth
can never periſh*. His owne, ſaid ſhee,
ſhall never periſh. Min. *But you are
one of thoſe Beſſie, and hath right to his
promiſe*. Shee anſwered, How ſhall I

be-

believe you who believeth not him who
hath all power, and is trueth it selfe? I
would faine seeke God, but I feele many stops and letts, and my prayers are
dung backe. If any had had foure and
twenty houres, yea, a touch of that, vnder which I haue lyne these three yeares,
they would thinke their case fearefull,
and would giue a world (if they had it)
for a blinck of his reconciled face: But
my calamitie will make others runne and
cry for mercy, my griefe and displeasure
is your joy and gladnesse. Min. *How
so Bessie, we take no pleasure in your grief.*
Shee answered, The Christian that is
sealed, seeing mee, will slie to mercy like
a bird, but I want wings.

After I had prayed for her, She sayes,
if God would giue mee a heart to giue
you thankes for your good prayer, I
would giue it: and if *I* had a motion in
the right way of saluation, O as *I* should
runne and slie to him like a bird. *GOD
bee blessed, said I, I see some fore-running
tokens of his comming with comfort.* She
answered, they are but sober and small
tokens. *Your words, said I, smels some-*
tymes

tymes of the Spirit of Grace and faith, and
sometimes of the flesh, infidelitie, and infirmitie: for the prayers of the Saincts are
oft like a fire, which at the first hath smoke
& reake, without light or heat, but break-
eth out ere all bee done in a cleare light,
and comfortable heat, as may bee seene in
sundrie of Davids Psalmes; where he be-
ginneth with heavie plaints, and endeth
in heavenly praises and prayers ere all be
done.

〈 At another time I speared if any comfort was yet come? Shee answered, Do-
lour was come, but no comfort, you are
troubled with mee in Pulpet, and out of
Pulpet, and in comming vnto me day after day: will you make you quite of this
cumber. Bessie said I, I thinke no cumber
of it, it is the duety of my calling, & would
God you got comfort by it: but how shall I
free my selfe of it. Shee answered, Cause
cut mee off. And wherefore said I, wold
you haue mee, or any taking your blood on
vs, and sinne on our sCules. Nay, no sinne
said shee, for there is just cause. What
cause, said I, What haue you done deser-
ving death? Is not vnbeliefe, said she-

B 5   th

the greatest sinne in the world, and I
am guiltie of it. *We haue, said I, no warrand for that: againe you are not voyde of
faith, how ever in your wrestling with vnbeliefe, you thinke so, and you would faine
believe, and bee freed of vnbeliefe, that
you might say with the Apostle, it is not
you* but sinne in you: *you are a sufferer in
this against your will: you are spiritually
oppressed, and groanes to God vnder this
bondage.* Then shee vttereth these
words, O that I could get that fountaine
of faith, a sterne of it! O as grace wold
grow! O for a blessed blinck of the fa-
vourable face of the Father of the faithfull! O to winne to that holy fountaine!
I know hee is readie to giue, if I were
readie to receaue and seeke: glorie per-
taineth to him, and glorified shall he be.
Min. I pray you Bessie seeke on, and glorifie him by incalling on his Name: pray
him in IESVS Name to bee mercifull to
you, and helpe your vnbeliefe. I can, said
shee, name IESVS, but hee will not be
pleased with words, except I had a warrand of faith in my heart to seeke by.
*Min. Yet will you say the words, I thinke
there*

there is none but you, but they wil doe this much for mee. Many speakes them, said shee, with little faith, but I dare not, that I draw not downe his punishments Min. *Bessie, hee will never bee angrie that you pray him to glorifie himselfe, in giving you an heart to believe in him.* I haue great letts, said shee. Min. *But pray him to take them away.* Thinke you, said she, that be to doe while now. Min. *But continue and let mee heare you and bee a witnesse to it, doe this for my pleasure.* It were my owne pleasure and good, said shee, if I could doe it rightly, it were my owne well: but God hath a worke to worke with mee, that you never saw the like of it.

Min. *Bessie, pray God in Iesus that it may bee a worke of mercy to his glorie and your salvation.* Shee answered, I will tell you my minde, IESVS is a just one without exception, not like the false flesh of this generation, hee will losse none of his owne, and though they fall fearefully he will raise them againe, but those that he bids not of, he giues them no grace to seeke to him, whereof I am one: I can

againe

name him and speake any words as you
heere, my mouth should bee opned to
speake, if my heart were opned to belieue,
but it is clofed, I may mourne for it, but
I cannot mend it, but LORD mend it,
LORD mend it. *Eeke said I, for Chrifts
fake.* I want faith, faid fhee, I know the
finne of man is not fo great, but GODS
mercie is greater to for-giue it,
where they can repent and belieue.
But I haue not this grace of my felfe, and
God gives mee it not: Pray that ye may
be preferved from the perill and plague
that is come on mee. Well is them that
are grounded on Chrift. Well is them
that are brethren and fifters to him. O
that I were one of them! O that thofe
that are come out of my loynes would
feeke to him, and bleffe him! O that the
Grace-giver would give mee grace to
believe and give him glory, and I fhould
bleffe him, and give him thankes and
praife and honour and glory for ever! O
that I could get an heart to give him
thankes for any thing hee fends. why
fhould not I be content with his will?
O that I could welcome his fend, howe
bitter

bitter foever, and reverence the fender?
What recks of mee; if hee get his owne
glory? but alace I have many wants, many woes, many wannes, wangrace, wan-
chance, no wealles: I am forely fhaken,
a fore fhake of wrath is come on my
foule.

MIN. *Hee fhakes you* Beffie *to make you
fure.* If it were fo faid fhee, I wold feeke
to him; The tentation (faid I) dings you
from that that you defire, and you are
greatly wounded in your fpirituall battell: But what recks of a wound to him
that getteth the victorie, you will in the
Lordes mercie get the victorie, what
reck of your wounds then: And we will
fitt downe on our knees and crave it to
you of God in the name of Iefus. After I
had prayed fhee fayeth, God for thy beloved fonne Iefus fake, fee to my mifter
and fuccour mee. Now yee are witnes
of that, that yee would have had, that I
feeke in Iefus name. Bleffed be God for
it faid I, Seeke on, and I will pledge my
foule for yours, that you fhall bee fafe.
Seeke muft I faid fhee, and feeke fhall I,
though hee fhould ding mee back to the.
bot-

bottome of the sea, & charge the whole
family that they doe the like, as you doe
mee, for come well, come woe, they will
get a share of it: I will (said I) for they
have to concurre with you.

The next time that I visited her, and
demanded how shee did, shee answered,
The life of the body is not like to goe
out, and comfort is not like to come in
to the soule: Yet waite Bessie in hope &
give not over, it will come. I know said
shee your tales and tydings, but cannot
find them true: alace that ever I came in
the world, I am not booked, I am not
baptized, I am not written in the booke
of Life, I am not baptized with the right
baptisme, I cannot finde the fruite of it.
Bessie said I, I am sorrie that I finde you
not as I left you: continued you not calling on God in Christs name, as you promised? Shee answered, I was the worse
of the words that you caused me to say;
I am ever since a thousand fold more tru-
bled than before. Bessie the words have
not the wyte: it's Satan that rageth before he be cast out, and your trouble the
neerer the height, the neerer is the deli-
veric.

verie, and althogh your Physick be bitter, yet it will have good effects. No trouble is joyous or pleasant for the present &c. Heb. 12. The Lord who will not let the hand of the wicked lye long on the backe of the righteous. Psal. 125. 3. will not let his owne hand which is heavier than the hand of the wicked lye long, he will send the issue with the tentation. 1. Cor. 10. 13. Wherfore hearken not Bessie to Satans suggestions that your heart bee not bound vp that you pray not: That is (said shee) a true tale, Satan binds vp my heart. But pray said I against it: say the Lords prayer. I can said shee saye the wordes, but I haue no warrant to pray it. I cannot call him Father, hee is the Father of the faithfull alone, but that priviledge of children is not given mee. I cannot finde a warrant that I am his, alace that ever I was the cursed ground whereon the ill seed was sowne.

Min. *Bessie, the more miserable you find your selfe, the more meet are you to goe to the Saviour for mercie.*

Bes. I am not said shee worthie that
bee

hee should give me any grace or mercie.
Min. *Beſſie, none is worthie, and if hee
gave to the worthie, his glory and praiſe
would bee the leſſe, but in this is his mercy
magnified, that he manifeſteth it on the
miſerable; and this a fault in vs, that wee
are ever ſeeking ſomething in our ſelves,
which would derogate from the praiſe of
his grace, as preſumption and deſperation
are dangerous rocks that manie runne on:
and this is a third and as dangerous as a-
ny of them, and the rather, that it is not
ſoone ſeene or tane vp, wee are aye ſeeking
ſomething in our ſelves that ſhould commend vs to God, as if we could not bee ſaved except wee were perfite, as if our owne
innocencie, and not Gods mercie in Chriſts
merite were the warrant of our ſalvation.*
Beſ. I cannot ſaid ſhee ſpeake the word
can pleaſe you, No, not them that came
out of my bowells, howe then can it
pleaſe the Lord? Mine owne minde and
Satan lets mee not believe, and my vnbeliefe draweth downe all the ill ofthe
word, and you booke mee, and carries
my name in many airts: but I cannot
mend it.

Min.

Min. Beſſie, nothing to your prejudice carie I your name, for whye ſhould not the Saints know of your eſtate?

Beſ. I pray you tell mee ſaid ſhee, how the people thinke of mee, whether are they blyth or woe?

Min. I will aſſure you Beſſie, Gods people mournes with you, and beares a part of your burthen, as for my ſelfe I haue fiue children ſick of the fever, God who knowes my heart, is my witnes, that I would not ſo faine haue them raiſed vp in their bodies, as you comforted in ſpirit.

Beſ. You know your reward, ſaid ſhee.

Min. I looke not to that, I ſeeke mercie.

Beſ. But ſaid ſhe, if I had ſpirituall grace and could, I would give you a reward. Will ever that day dawne that G O D will draw mee a wandring ſheepe home to himſelfe?

Min. Beſſie, in Gods mercie I am aſſured of it.

Beſ. The God ſaid ſhee who made heaven & earth, who hath all power grant it in mercy; weale is them for ever finds his favour, but woe is them that feeles his ſead: had I hope it wold mitigat my
ſor-

sorrow.

Min. Bessie said I, the Lord who by a secret grace vnderproppes & sustaines you, now will in his owne time, by a sensible grace, and by his felt presence aboundantly comfort your soule in such sort, that the weight and grievousnesse of the tentation and trouble and delay of time, shall bee recompensed with vnspeakable joy, that you your self shall confesse, the one light in regard of the other, not to bee worthie of it: as by the contrare, hee recompenseth the delaye of judgment towards the wicked, with the heavier weight of wrath.

Bes. Happie (said shee) are they who suffer for Christs sake, for righteousnesse sake, they will bee comforted now and then: but they that suffer for sinne, without sense of his favour, comfortlesse is their condition. Will one goe through the earth, vp and down, to & fro, where will they find a wearied wight till they come to mee. And you that heare mee, with the pith of prayer that *I* can, I aske of God that yee never know the waye that *I* am in: *It* is lacke of faith that is my losse, want of faith is my wracke, I

lye

ly vnder fearefull weights, and wanteth faith to get the remiſſion of them. I am fallen without a reſurrection: My Iudge is my partie: I have no claime to his mercie: I have no ground of faith to faſten grips on him: I find not a ſparke of light, and I find no fruit of your prayers, albeit I heare them: No Chriſtian ſhould come neere mee.

Min. *Beſſie, The LORD will oft for good cauſes deſert his deareſt Sainčts, and withdraw himſelfe from their ſight and ſenſe, for their humiliation and inſtruction, (that they count not grace naturall) for their greater cōſolation When he cōmeth againe: & for your provocation to follow after him when he withdrawes his grace, and yet it is not a reall, but a ſuppoſed deſertion: Wherefore ſeeke his ſenſible preſence, and breake thorow all impediments of terrour, blindneſſe, and vnbelieſe, or what elſe, thrimble thorow all, and hee ſhall come leaping over the mountaines of your ſinnes and hilles of wrath, with the voyce of heavenly conſolation.*

Beſ. Shall I ſeeke hote water vnder cold yce: I haue not come in the preciſe

cise and blessed houre of grace: I am
come behinde, and where you will mee
to pray, wherefore serues the prayer that
glorifieth not God.

Min. *Bessie, It is yet the acceptable
time, and hee Who is found of them that
seeke him not, will much more reveale himselfe to them who secketh.   And as for
prayer, by it you greatly glorifie God: for
you acknowledge therein your miserie, and
necessitie, and that hee is GOD who not
onely knowes your miserie, and necessitie,
but is both willing and able to helpe the
same, and wee haue not only his command
to pray, but also his promise to bee heard.*

Bes. Then all breake his command,
and chiefly I, and so will be seene on the
whole swacke,

After this, when I had read some comfortable places to her, and prayed for
her, shee cryed out and doubled
it oft: O blessed are they
that have that spirit of
prayer! O blessed
are they!

NOW

NOW as for the end of this conflict, and death of this deare daughter of *Abraham*, in Apryle 1625. I beeing in *Glasgow* at the provinciall assemblie, the LORD called her home, shee being greatly extenuate and worne, what by heavie sicknesse on her bodie, what by this longsome and fearefull exercise in her soule: death on a suddaintie delt with her heart, that her words and speach failed her: but in presence of diverse witnesse, her hands and eyes were heaved to the heavens, and so giving that signe of victorie, shee randered her spirit: and although it pleased not our gratious GOD (who in his great wisedome worketh after diverse sortes with his owne) to let vs heare out of her owne mouth of the glorious victorie, and vnspeakeable joyes that he had given her inwardly in her soule, yet I am sure there is none that is illuminate from aboue, & taught to discerne spiritually, that will any way dout of her blessed deliverāce, albeit no outward signe had bene seene: yea, it was a wonderfull mercie, that

God

God so long vnder such horrours, held
her owne hand out of her selfe. Which
at last with her eyes shee lifted vp to the
Heavens, when her speach could not expresse her inward feeling of an vnspeakable joy, and victorious faith.

Onely heerein wee haue our warning
to bee wise in time, and to get oyle into
our Lampes, and not to please our selues
with toome Lampes, and with a bare
show of an outward profession, but labour to haue a liuely and effectuall
faith, in the deepe of our soules for
a conceit or opinion will seeme
sufficient till wee bee put at,
which will not doe our
turne, nor stand vs
in stead in the
firie tryall.

FINIS.